MW00472047

BEYOND THE FARTHEST STAR

A Novel

Dee Dee Chumley

www.gsg.biz

Copy Right © 2011 by Dee Dee Chumley

All rights reserved. Except as permitted under the U.S. Copyright Act of 1976, no part of this publication may be reproduced, distributed, or transmitted in any form or by any means, or stored in a database or retrieval system, without the prior written permission of the publisher.

G.IS.G Heavenly Publications

21050 Little Beaver Rd, Apple Valley, CA 92308

Visit our Web site at www.gisg.biz

First Edition: December 2011

G.IS.G Heavenly Publications is a division of G.IS.G, LLC.

G.IS.G Heavenly Publications name and logo are trademarks of G.IS.G, LLC.

The characters and events portrayed in this book are fictitious. Any similarity to real persons, living or dead, is coincidental and not intended by the author.

ISBN-13: 978-1478326106

ISBN-10: 1478326107

Printed in the United States of America

10 9 8 7 6 5 4 3 2 1

Dedication

To Kristin and all the *Darcys* who graced my
classroom and inspired this story.

Acknowledgements

Because a lifetime of experiences goes into any book, it is hard to acknowledge everyone who played a part in it. But a few deserve my special thanks: my parents, Joe and Gladys Fink, who instilled in me a love for reading; my writing group—Kelly Bristow, Martha Bryant, Lisa Marotta, Sonia Gensler, Shel Harrington, Karen Cooper, and Karuna Clark—who provided critiquing, insight, and encouragement; Kristin Lusk, Lacy Hay, Jordyn Poston, and Jessie Nowakowski, who served as my test readers; and Sarah Basore and the people of God is Good Heavenly Publications, who believed in this book and its message. I'm particularly indebted to two individuals: Bill, who encouraged me more than he knew by introducing me as "...my wife, a writer"; and Brandi Barnett, who opened a whole new world to me with the question, "Would you like to join our writing group?" Such caring, supportive people remind me daily that God truly is good.

BEYOND THE FARTHEST STAR

A Novel

CHAPTER ONE

Tiffin Griffith reminded Darcy of the Barbie stored under her bed. Both had dyed black hair, heavy eye make-up, a painted-on tan, and synthetic boobs. But suggesting the two were similar was unfair...to Barbie.

Unlike Tiffin, the doll wasn't deadly.

Today Darcy stood two people behind Tiffin in the *D-G* line and waited to pick up her class schedule. Tiffin whispered to her friend Angie and then cast sinister looks in Darcy's direction. Darcy strained to listen. She didn't consider this eavesdropping. She considered it survival.

In middle school, Tiffin's bullying almost cost Darcy her life. Six years later, sound bites of her conversation—"...sick and tired...putting an end to it...has it coming...could get hurt"—indicated Tiffin still had plans to carry out.

"Hey, Dars! Over here!"

Darcy saw her best friend Megan waving her own schedule in the air.

"I'll have mine in a minute," Darcy shouted back. She pointed toward the commons. "Wait for me by the stairs."

Moments later, Darcy and Megan compared schedules. "We have only one class together," Megan complained, "but at least it's homeroom. We can plan lunch the first thing every morning."

The two friends usually tag-teamed their conversations, one jumping in the moment the other paused to breathe. But today, as they walked down the hallway, Megan did all the talking. In the classroom Darcy half-heartedly greeted some friends and plunked down in a desk a respectable distance from the front row.

Megan claimed the desk behind her. "I thought this day would

1

never come," she said to the back of Darcy's head. "I'm so ready for our senior year. How about you?"

Darcy twisted around. "Yeah, I guess I'm ready."

"That's it? You *guess* you're ready? Last night you couldn't stop talking about it. You had your calendar filled for the first three months." She wrinkled her forehead. "What's up with you?"

Darcy shrugged and faced forward again. Until today she had shared her friend's excitement over their last year in high school. Tiffin's words this morning had changed all that.

"Hey, Taylor…hi, Donna!"

The skin on the back of Darcy's neck prickled. Only two possible sources could produce such an irritating sound: out-of-tune bagpipes or Tiffin's shrieks.

The entire class looked toward the doorway where Tiffin executed a beauty-pageant wave and flashed her toothy smile—another feature she shared with Barbie. Tiffin's boyfriend Reese loomed behind her like a dark cloud searching for something to rain on.

Mrs. Perkins arranged the papers on her podium. "I was about to call roll," she said to Easton High's most infamous couple. "You're already late. Please hurry and take a seat."

Tiffin tilted her head to the side and jutted her chin forward. Now she talked in a babyish voice and with a lisp she had somehow acquired over the summer. "Oh, I'm so sorry, Mrs. Perkins." She resumed her smile and clumped across the tile floor in her platform heels. Reese sauntered close behind.

Megan leaned forward and whispered again to Darcy. "I know Tiffin's not exactly National Merit material, but she can't be that dumb. What does she see in that creeper?"

"Beats me. Maybe she has a thing for short boys with zits."

"Yeah. And boys shaped like a Hummer."

Darcy snickered. Reese used to be a nice guy. Over the last couple of years, though, he had grown moody. In less time than it takes a traffic light to change, he could go from charmer to jerk. And he had a reputation for picking fights.

A wave of panic washed over Darcy when Tiffin and Reese passed her desk. Now that she had a few more years experience—and with some pointers from Reese—Tiffin could be more ruthless than she had been in middle school.

In sixth grade Darcy narrowly escaped disaster with the help of an old lady who appeared out of nowhere. Today she doubted another guardian angel would come to her rescue.

"Heads up! Major hottie at ten o'clock!"

CHAPTER TWO

In response to Megan's excited whisper, Darcy looked up. Her jaw dropped and all thoughts of Tiffin's treachery vanished. In the doorway, stood the certifiably best-looking guy Darcy had ever seen.

Every pair of eyes in the room—male as well as female—focused on the figure. It wasn't just his movie-star looks. Something indefinable about him drew responses ranging from curiosity to awe.

"Sorry," he said to Mrs. Perkins. "I'm new here. Had a little trouble finding the room."

The new boy made his way between the rows and sat at the desk next to Darcy. "Hi, I'm Mike…Mike Albright," he said to her. He spoke with confidence rarely found in guys his age and he wore his smile as comfortably as most boys wear their favorite ball caps.

"H…hi, I…I'm Darcy." She cringed at her wimpy response. Get a grip, girl. You've seen cute guys before. And for heaven's sake, close your mouth. Next thing you know you'll be drooling. Darcy faced away from Mike to hide the red splotches she felt creeping up her neck.

When Mike turned to introduce himself to another student, Megan grilled Darcy. "What's wrong with you? The most gorgeous hunk in the history of Easton High chooses a seat next to you and introduces himself and you don't talk to him?"

Darcy couldn't answer Megan because she didn't know what was wrong with her. She talked to boys all the time and never had a problem finding something to say. With Mike, she had barely been able to put three words together.

Anyway, Mike Albright wasn't all that hot. Sure, he was tall and ripped and had a nice smile, but look at the way he dressed: scruffy athletic shoes, baggy tee shirt, rumpled jeans. Of course, she did like the way those rumples smoothed out over his—

"Oh. My. Gosh." Megan's eyes grew wide at her discovery. "Darcy Dunn, the queen of composure, has finally met someone who leaves her speechless."

"Don't be—"

Megan held up her hand, palm forward. "No, don't deny it. You can't fool me. The girl who has always guarded her heart like it was a national treasure just had it stolen." She beamed with satisfaction. "And to think I witnessed the whole thing."

"Forget it, Megan. You're hallucinating." She had to put an end to this line of talk right away. If she didn't, Megan would have Mike and her engaged to be married by sixth hour.

At home, she lugged her pile of books through the kitchen door and dropped them on the nearest flat surface. Sweaty strands of hair stuck to her face. Her skin felt as gritty as sandpaper. First day of the school year over, one-hundred-eighty-four to go.

She greeted her dad and Rufus, her rescued pound puppy who refused to stop yapping until she acknowledged him. "Hey, Rufie. Hey, boy." She patted his head and rubbed behind his ears. "Yeah, yeah, I'm glad to see you, too."

She opened the fridge and took out a Coke. "Whew! Feels good in here. Practice was a killer today." She took off her drenched cap and held the cold bottle against her cheek. "Ahhh. That feels good. Must be at least 110 outside."

Chet Dunn peered through the window at the patio thermometer. "It's only 107. You're such a whiner." He gave her a wink as he sprinkled seasoning over steaks.

"Yeah, well, that's in the shade." She pulled out a chair and sat down at the kitchen table. "Stand in the middle of a tennis court and check the temperature there."

Her dad picked up a plate piled with meat and headed out to the grill. A few minutes later, he stepped back inside. "Steaks will be done in ten minutes. About the time your mother gets home."

Darcy gulped the last of her Coke. "Anything I can do?"

Her dad sat down at the table. "Nope, everything's ready. How was practice today besides being hot?"

"Good. My backhand volley still needs work, but my ground strokes are smoking."

"Atta girl. What about school? How was the first day of your senior year?"

"Okay, I guess."

Her dad laced his fingers behind his neck and stretched out his long legs. "Not a lot of enthusiasm there. I thought you were excited about this year."

Darcy chewed her lip and didn't respond right away. She couldn't tell him that now, instead of looking forward to her senior year, she wanted only to finish it and get as far away from Tiffin as possible.

Words from a song she'd heard kept running through her head: "beyond the farthest star." To Darcy it sounded like the perfect place to escape from Tiffin and all the trouble she caused.

But her dad would never approve of running away from anything or anybody. His years in management had trained him to "get to the root of the problem" and "determine the best possible solution."

Rather than risk a pep talk, she changed the subject. "I'm gross from practice. Think I have time for a quick shower?"

He sniffed the air, then held his nose. "Please. Take all the time you need."

After dinner that evening, she sat in her room and attacked her homework. Off to a great start. The first day of school and already she was drowning in assignments. She worked for a while but her mind kept wandering. When her phone rang, she answered before checking the caller's name. Talking to anybody was better than conjugating Spanish verbs.

"Hello."

"Well, what do you think?" Megan never bothered with preliminaries.

"About what?"

"You know about what. The new guy."

"Haven't given him much thought."

"Sure you haven't. I heard the way you got all tongue-tied around him. I know something was bothering you this morning, but you're not dead."

Not yet, Darcy thought.

* * * *

"Sir, it's great to hear from you." In a house on the outskirts of town, Mike spoke with affection.

7

"Same here," Col. Michael said. "I want to hear all about your first day in Easton. How did it go?"

"Not too bad. It's always a little rocky the first few days in a new place, but, by now, I've learned the rough spots eventually smooth out."

"That's true. And making friends and fitting in has never been a problem for you. Still, I hate it that service life causes us so much upheaval. Unfortunately, Mike, there's no way to avoid it."

"Yes, sir, I know that." Touched by a longing for home, Mike tried to sound upbeat, but he couldn't mask his loneliness. New assignments always meant separation, and by now he should be used to it. But while others might welcome long-term breaks from the supervision of loved ones, he didn't. Each time, he felt as shaky as a baby bird shoved from the nest.

The colonel tried to reassure him. "Even though we're apart for a while, you're never deserted. And you don't have to solve all the world's problems by yourself. Help is always available. Don't be afraid to ask for it."

Before signing off, Col. Michael repeated the importance of this current mission. He emphasized his final words. "Remember, failure to obtain its objectives could mean the difference between life and death."

CHAPTER THREE

"You might as well save yourself some grief and give in," Darcy said to Chad. "You're going to lose."

At lunch on Tuesday, Darcy, Megan, and Chad sat at a table at Taco Grande with the rest of the group: Cliff, Susan, Lacey and Chris. They had all been friends since middle school, where they christened themselves the Lucky Seven. For convenience the name was shortened to the Sevens, but the friendships had lasted throughout high school.

Chad shook his head. "Forget it, Megan. What you're asking me to do is lame. Guys do not—I repeat, *do not*—ask other guys to dances."

Chris and Cliff nodded their agreement.

Megan ignored them. Although she stood only five feet tall, her determination more than made up for her lack of height. "Don't be so homophobic," she said. "In the course of a conversation with Mike, you mention there's always a Howdy Dance the first Friday after school starts. Then you explain a bunch of us meet there, hang out together, and would like for him to join us." Megan talked fast so Chad wouldn't have a chance to object. "It's no big deal. That way Darcy will know if he'll be at the dance and can plan accordingly."

Darcy snapped to attention. "Whoa! Don't drag me into this. I never said anything about wanting Mike Albright to come to the dance."

"Of course, you didn't," Megan said. "You're too busy wallowing in your back-to-school funk to notice Mike is perfect for you." Her gaze circled the table, coming to a rest on Chad. "Why am I the only one who realizes that?"

"Okay, okay." Chad held up both hands. "I give up. I'll try to find some way to bring up the subject without sounding like I'm asking him for a date. Geez, Meg, I don't know why I let you talk me into these things."

Darcy knew why. With her big brown eyes and little button nose, Megan could have the persuasive powers of a cocker spaniel puppy. Nobody could say no to a face like that.

Back at school, Megan pushed and shoved both Chad and Darcy through the crowded hallway so they could "accidentally" run into Mike.

"How do you know where his fifth hour is?" Darcy asked, still not sold on this idea.

"I found out yesterday. I went to the counseling office and told them I had to deliver him a note from his sister."

"He has a sister?"

Megan rolled her eyes. "How should I know?"

Megan was giving Chad last minute instructions on how to sound casual and unrehearsed when they spotted Mike's head above the crowd of students. With Chad and Darcy in tow, Megan elbowed her way over to Mike.

Megan introduced Chad and then shoved Darcy toward Mike. "And you remember Darcy from homeroom."

"Hi, again," Darcy said, her mind racing. She wasn't trying to think of something clever to say. She was trying to think of *anything* to say.

Megan jumped in, breaking the awkward silence. "We were wondering if you knew about the school's Howdy Dance on Friday night."

"No, I haven't heard—"

"Hi, Mike!" The tapping of high heels accompanied the screech. Tiffin ran up to the group and wedged her body between Mike and the others. With no apology for disrupting the previous conversation, she started one of her own. "I wanted to let you know about a party on Friday night."

"Yeah," Mike said. "The Howdy Dance. Megan was telling—"

"No, I wasn't talking about that." Tiffin tilted her head backward, indicating the group behind her. "Unless you want to hang out with losers all night."

"Excuse me—" Megan began but stopped when Darcy whirled around and charged down the hall.

"Wait!" Megan yelled. "Where are you going?"

"I don't want to be late for class," Darcy called over her shoulder.

Megan ran and caught up with her. "Wait a minute! Why are you running away? We haven't said anything to Mike yet."

"Looks to me like Mike has other plans for Friday night." Darcy tried to keep on walking, but Megan blocked her path.

"You don't know that. You didn't wait to hear his answer. Do you think Tiffin is Mike's kind of girl? I mean, look at them."

Darcy forced herself to watch the scene unfolding between Tiffin and Mike. Tiffin stood not two inches from Mike and rested her hand on his chest. She ogled him like some rock-star groupie, and Darcy heard her say, "Please say you'll come."

Megan's face twisted in disgust. "Doesn't she know Mike's way too nice for her? For one thing, her in-your-face attitude makes him so nervous he hardly knows how to act. . And I can't imagine him at a field party, can you?"

Darcy was about to agree with Megan when she saw Tiffin give Mike's arm a squeeze. Then Tiffin licked her lips and said loud enough for Darcy and everyone within a twenty-mile radius to hear, "I'll guarantee you a good time."

Darcy closed her eyes and slowly shook her head. "Let it go. I'm not in the mood for this." She shoved past Megan and tromped toward her next class.

After sixth hour, she hurried to her car in the student parking lot . She slowed her pace when she saw who was waiting there. "Here we go again," she muttered.

Looking like a parent ready to deliver a lecture, Megan leaned against Darcy's car, her arms folded across her chest. "You know what your trouble is? You're never in the mood to stand up to Tiffin. How can you stand to see her—"

"What do you want from me?" Darcy shouted. "You heard her. How am I supposed to compete with a come-on like that? Mike's cute, but I'm not so desperate that I'm willing to guarantee *any* boy a good time."

"It's not that," Megan said. "Of course I don't expect you to compete with Tiffin in that way. But for six years, I've watched you back down to that tramp. For six years, she's played every dirty trick in the book on you, and you ignore her or go out of your way to avoid her.

Why did you let her shove you out of the way today? Why did you let her take over the conversation?"

Students walking to their cars gawked as Megan's voice grew louder. "I don't understand you. You tackle schoolwork, tennis…everything you do with bulldog determination. I've never seen you back down from any challenge…except Tiffin. Sometimes I'd swear you're afraid of her."

Darcy's pulse pushed against her eardrums. She took a deep breath and began mentally counting to ten. At five she said, "Maybe I back down to Tiffin because she never fights fair. She should have a black belt in cheating and lying. I might be a wuss, but I'm not stupid. I know a no-win situation when I see one."

The frown lines across Megan's forehead smoothed, and her clamped jaw relaxed. "You're right about Tiffin," she said. "But you can't run from her forever. You've got to find a way to deal with her." Megan took three steps, then stopped and stretched to her full five feet before delivering her pronouncement. "Six years is long enough."

Darcy plunked behind the wheel of her car and drove to the tennis courts for after-school practice, steaming over Megan's accusations. Megan had never been Tiffin's designated victim. She had no idea the effects of Tiffin's cruelty went way beyond bruised feelings or shattered self-confidence. In middle-school, Tiffin's bullying had been dangerous but, in high school, it had more or less downgraded to annoying. Darcy learned a long time ago fighting with Tiffin only made matters worse, so she had gone through the last few years ignoring her when possible. Evidently that hadn't solved the problem. It had only postponed it.

Meagan didn't know about Tiffin's latest threat. The words Darcy overheard in the line yesterday caused old fears, as well as a new one, to surface. The fear that this time she wouldn't survive Tiffin's reign of terror.

CHAPTER FOUR

The first rule of tennis: Keep your eye on the ball. In sixth grade, Darcy learned a sure-fire way to do that. Picturing Tiffin's fake smile on the ball assured she made solid contact with it. That year, she won the middle-school state championship. Today, with every shot she hit, Tiffin received a resounding whack right in her collagen-inflated lips.

"Hey, Dunn!" Coach Davis shouted from the next court, mock disapproval on his face. "Take it easy on those practice balls. They have to last us all season."

"Sorry, Coach." She tossed a ball into the air and blasted it into the opposing service court.   After practice, she pulled into the driveway of her house. The grueling workout had exhausted her, but it had also calmed her. . She called Megan on her cell phone.

"Hey, I'm sorry about our fight this afternoon."

"What fight?"

"Mmm...let me think...the one that half the kids in the parking lot overheard?"

"That was a fight? That was a friend giving helpful advice."

Darcy laughed. "It was pretty loud advice."

"I guess it was. Look, I'm sorry. You probably have good reasons for avoiding Tiffin. She can be vicious. But you know you can always count on me and the Sevens to back you."

"I know. Thanks."

Darcy put away her phone and went into the house. She had the best friends in the world. They would do anything for her. But would that be enough to protect her from Tiffin?

Wednesday after school, Darcy walked to her locker before tennis practice. Her face grew warm as Mike fell in step beside her. This time, though, she was determined to act as if she had talked to a boy before.

She wouldn't be struck dumb by his slightly crooked smile or perfect teeth or eyes the color of rich chocolate.

"Now that we're two days into the school year, how's it going for you?" Mike asked.

"Let's say about like I expected." Her heart thumped against the front of her shirt. She wondered if he could see it. "How about you? Feel like a genuine Easton Eagle yet?"

"Well, that could take some time."

"Oh, yeah?"

"I'm a pretty slow learner, and it takes a navigational system to find the way around this place. Besides that, my second hour is in the math hallway, and my third hour is in the history wing." He held up a map of the school. "Do you know a secret to making it from one end of this school to the other in less than five minutes?"

She pretended to study the map while she considered asking Mike to the dance. Perhaps Megan was right. Maybe he hadn't accepted Tiffin's invitation to the field party. Now would be the perfect opportunity to find out.

"Darcy! Could I speak to you a minute?" Coach Davis called to her from across the hall.

Darn it! Her coach had rotten timing. "Yes, sir," she said and apologized to Mike.

"That's okay. But never accuse guys of not asking for directions."

Over the next two days, Darcy waited for another chance to mention the upcoming dance to Mike, but a subtle way to do it didn't present itself.

"Why be subtle?" Megan asked at lunch on Friday. "Come right out with it. You're not asking him to marry you, for Pete's sake. You're asking him to a dance. I'll never understand why you're so uptight about this sort of thing."

"And I can never understand how you're so upfront about everything."

Megan dipped a chicken nugget into sweet and sour sauce. "I might be upfront, but at least I'd know if Mike was coming to the dance tonight."

That evening, Darcy faced a wardrobe dilemma. Like most girls her age, she liked clothes, but unlike them, she hated to shop. The dance tonight wasn't a big dress-up occasion, but she wanted to look good for

14

the first all-school party of the year. She admitted she also wanted to look good on the slim chance Mike showed up. Now she wished when she'd shopped for back-to-school clothes, she'd taken the time to buy something other than jeans.

She rummaged through her closet and came across an outfit she had bought this summer for vacation. The khaki shorts were cool and comfortable, and the burnt-orange tunic almost glowed against her tanned skin. The cafeteria would be sweltering, so she pulled her sun-streaked hair straight back in a ponytail and wore very little makeup.

At the school, the air vibrated with rap and rock music, and students crowded every nook and cranny of the cafeteria. Darcy knew this dance always attracted swarms of students who weren't necessarily glad to be back at school but were glad to be back at school parties.

She and Megan stood near the doorway with Cliff and Chad and scanned the crowd for Mike.

Megan stood on her tiptoes and shouted over the noise. "Do you see him?"

Darcy shook her head.

"Well, keep a lookout. He might show up later." Megan grabbed Chad's hand and dragged him onto the dance floor.

Cliff turned to Darcy. "Wanna dance?" He was already moving to the beat of the music.

"Mmm, no thanks. I'm going to get something to drink and talk to a couple of friends. You go ahead."

"I'll save you one," Cliff said and hurried away to find another partner.

For the next half hour, Darcy stood around talking to friends, frequently checking the entrance. When Mike didn't show up, she joined in the dancing.

CHAPTER FIVE

Tiffin had been attending these field parties for what seemed like forever. When she was in eighth grade, she thought they were exciting and considered herself special when a Hawk invited her to one. Every student from sixth grade up knew the Hawks were the coolest kids in school.

But now the parties were boring, the same thing over and over. The Hawks gathered in a location unknown to school officials or the police. Someone's older brother or sister or sometimes parents provided the "refreshments"—booze and pot—and entertainment consisted of loud talking and listening to ear-splitting music. Those who had dates lay on blankets on the fringes of the group or stayed in their cars making out.

Tonight was the kick-off party for the school year. Guys stood around in groups telling lies about their athletic abilities or romantic conquests. Girls tried to impress the boys by cursing and seeing how drunk or stoned they could get.

Reese and Tiffin sat entangled in Reese's huge truck.

"C'mon, baby. You know I love you." Reese whined like a two-year-old. "Don't you love me?"

"Yes."

"Then show me. It's not like we ain't done this before. Why're you so mean to me tonight?" Reese started to reach under her shirt.

"Because it seems like this is all you ever want to do anymore. Why can't we go to any of the school dances or any parties besides field parties?" Tiffin tried to re-direct Reese's roving hands. "And even at these, I can't talk to my friends. All we do is sit in your truck and...well, you know."

"You never complained before. What's different now?"

Her body stiffened when Reese tightened his grip on her waist. "Nothing."

"Well, that's good, baby." He grabbed a handful of hair and jerked her head back. "Because if—"

"Ow, let go! You're drunk, and you're hurting me!" She struggled to free herself, but he held firm and stuck his face within an inch of hers.

"Because if you're losin' interest, I—" He looked up. "What the ...?"

A beat-up, white pickup rattled into the field, its headlights blazing.

"Who is that moron?" Reese shaded his eyes with his hands and squinted. "I don't recognize that piece of crap, and what's he doing with his lights on high beam? Why don't he take out an ad in the paper and announce where we're at?"

Mike turned off the engine, stepped out of his truck, and walked over to the startled Hawks and their dates. He greeted them all with a nod or *hey, man*. Most of the girls smiled at him and returned his greeting. The guys stood motionless, making no effort to welcome this uninvited guest.

Reese sat up straight behind his steering wheel and let loose with a string of obscenities. "What the hell is he doing here? How'd he find out about this?"

He eyed Tiffin. "You know anything about this?"

"No. Maybe." She avoided his accusing glare. "I might've mentioned something to him."

"Are you outta your mind? For all you know, that guy could be an undercover cop! There's something about him I don't trust." He doubled up his fist and hit the dashboard.

Tiffin flinched. "Don't be ridiculous. He's that new guy in our homeroom. He hasn't made many friends yet, so I thought—"

"I *know* who he is, okay? Do me a favor. Shut up. If you say one more word, I swear I'll—"

Mike tapped on the window. Hissing like an overheated radiator, Reese lowered his window.

Mike leaned down and peered into the cab. "Hi, Reese, hi, Tiffin. I'm glad I found you. I wasn't sure I was at the right place."

Reese opened the door and got out of his truck. "Oh, you

definitely *ain't* at the right place," he grumbled. He gave Mike a shove as he walked past him. Grabbing a beer from an ice chest, he popped the top and downed half the drink in one gulp. Then he leaned against another truck and glowered at Mike and Tiffin.

Tiffin gave Mike a nervous smile. "I'm glad you came. I wasn't sure you could make it." She tugged her shirt into place. "Could you give me a ride home? I'm kind of tired, and I think Reese is gonna be here for a long time."

"Sure thing." He waited for Tiffin to smooth her hair and check her make-up. Then he accompanied her across the field to his pickup. Neither of them dared to look back at Reese.

On the way to her house Tiffin sat in the middle of the seat, close to Mike.

"So is Reese your boyfriend?" Mike asked. "I see you with him a lot at school."

"I guess so. We've been goin' out since tenth grade, and I like him and all, but sometimes I think I'd like to date someone new." She snuggled closer and put her hand on Mike's thigh.

When he placed his hand on top of hers, a tingle of excitement shot through her. Then he brushed her hand aside and replaced his on the steering wheel. He stared straight ahead at the road. "Give me the directions to your house," he said. "I know you're tired and so am I. We'd better get home."

She frowned and sat up straight. It wasn't often she got that kind of response to her advances, but she wasn't giving up. She knew how to handle shy boys. Mike would come around.

She directed him to her house. A porch light was on, but not a single light came from inside.

"Will your parents be waiting up for you?" he asked.

"No, it's just me and my mom. On Friday nights, if she's not on a date, she's out partying with friends."

He pulled into the drive and kept the motor idling.

"You want to come in?" she asked, giving Mike her most enticing smile. "Have a beer? Watch a movie?"

"I'd better not tonight. But thanks." He reached across her and unlatched the passenger-door handle. "Sometimes this thing sticks," he explained. When she made no motion to leave, he said, "I'll wait here until you're in the house."

"That's so sweet of you." She gave him a peck on the cheek and got out of the truck. At her front door, she turned and waved.

* * * *

Mike returned the wave and backed out of the driveway. Driving through the older addition, he saw big houses with sprawling, manicured lawns. Tiffin's house was also large. But it needed repairs, the grass was overgrown, and the flowerbeds were full of weeds.

When he passed a black truck parked on the side of the road, the driver pulled out and tailed him. Mike didn't have to guess who the driver was. Reese rode Mike's bumper all the way to an old farmhouse five miles from town. Mike turned in his driveway and cut the engine. He watched in his rearview mirror as the truck continued on its way.

CHAPTER SIX

On Monday, the whole school was still talking about the dance: how much fun it was, who was there, who they danced with. Looking back, Darcy realized she had enjoyed herself once she stopped looking for Mike.

In homeroom Mike sat sideways in the desk in front of her. "So how was your weekend?"

She told him about the dance on Friday. "I thought you might be there."

"Mmm, I guess I'm still a little uncomfortable about being in a new school."

She found that surprising and a little hard to believe. From what she'd seen, he adjusted easily to new situations.

Tiffin and Reese came in and walked toward their seats, Tiffin in front. Mike glanced up at her, and Tiffin gave him a conspiratorial grin. Reese scowled more than usual.

Mike turned back to Darcy. "By the way, I have a date for lunch today."

This news should be of no concern to her, but Darcy couldn't stand not asking. "With Tiffin?"

"No. Why would you think that?"

The answer filled Darcy with relief, but now she was trapped. She tried to sound casual. "Well, who then? Anyone I know?"

"Yeah, I think so. Do you know a Megan Reynolds?"

Megan! Darcy might have known. She saw through the scheme right away. Megan, tired of waiting on Darcy, had taken matters into her own hands. The Sevens met for lunch on Mondays, so Megan devised this plan to get Darcy and Mike together. Sometimes, Megan's interfering irritated her. Today, she was grateful for her friend's meddling.

"There's one problem," Mike said.

"What's that?"

He nodded toward Megan. "I think you need to give your friend a lesson in manners. She asked me to lunch, then said she couldn't give me a ride. Pretty rude, huh?"

"Unforgivable."

"Well, since she's your friend, I think you should solve the problem."

"What do you have in mind?"

He placed his index finger on his lips and pretended to consider the question. "I can drive, but I don't know the way to The Tasty Treat. Could you go with me and give directions?"

"It's a big inconvenience, but I think I can manage," she said playfully. Then she looked back at Megan who was giving her a thumbs-up.

On the way to The Tasty Treat, Mike said, "So why would you think Tiffin and I had a date for lunch?"

Rats. Darcy thought she got away with that. "You aren't from anywhere around here, are you?" she asked.

A look of alarm crossed his face then vanished. "No. How'd you know?"

"The way you talk. Most kids in Oklahoma—heck, most adults for that matter—are pronoun challenged. You know, we say, 'Me and her are going to lunch,' or when we want to sound smart, we say something like 'between you and I.'" She leaned against the passenger door and faced him. "Even if we know the rules, we don't like to use them unless we're talking to our English teachers. It makes us sound like we care about grammar, and around here that's about as cool as playing the accordion."

Mike assumed a *Dukes of Hazard* accent. "Thanks, li'l lady. That's good advice. Anything else I need to know about livin' in these here parts so I don't stick out like a rooster in the hen house?"

"Well, first of all, our grammar might be a little strange, but it doesn't mean we keep our washing machines on the front porch and marry our cousins. So if I were you, I'd drop the Boss Hogg act. People might think you're making fun of them."

He smiled and dropped the accent. "Thanks. Some more good

advice. What else can you tell me about Easton?"

"I'd be glad to fill you in on a lot, but we're almost there." She pointed ahead. "Turn right at the next light and go one block. The Tasty Treat is on the left."

He gave a turn signal and eased into the right lane.

At The Tasty Treat, Darcy and Mike joined her friends at an outdoor picnic table. . On Mondays, the fast food restaurant offered a hamburger, French fries, and drink for $3.50, so the Sevens always met there on the first school day of the week, weather permitting.

Darcy introduced Mike to the Sevens he hadn't met. They all sat around one of the tables, chowing down on their hamburgers, tossing food at each other, and discussing teachers and classes. In response to their questions, Mike gave his observations on Easton High so far. He confessed the school was a lot larger than he'd expected, but he found most of the students and the faculty friendly.

The dance on Friday night came up. All agreed it had been a successful opening event.

Cliff licked ketchup off his thumb. "Speaking of opening events, I hear the Hawks hosted their season opener."

"No surprise there," Lacey said, handing him a napkin. "I don't think it was their season opener, though. I'm not sure the Hawks' party season ever ends."

Cliff laid the napkin on the table and continued to lick his fingers. "Yeah, but I heard they had some uninvited guests Friday night."

"Who?" Susan asked.

"The police." Cliff watched their surprised faces, clearly pleased he had aroused everyone's curiosity. "I think the party was almost over by the time they showed up. They didn't do much. Rounded up the drunks and told the rest to go home."

Megan reached across Chad for some salt. "I wonder how the cops found them."

"Mmm, I overheard Reese talking about it," Cliff said, "and he thinks he has a pretty good idea. You got any ideas, Mike?"

Everyone stopped chewing and gawked at Cliff as if he had spoken in Swahili. How would Mike know anything?

"I don't know," Mike said. "By the time the police arrived, I was long gone."

Like they were attached to the same string, every head swiveled toward Mike. He explained that Tiffin told him sometimes a group of her friends got together on weekends to relax and hang out. She asked him to join them. He had no idea who the Hawks were or what they did until last Friday night.

Holding his hamburger in one hand and a French fry in the other, Mike shrugged. "Who knew? When I got there, I figured out pretty fast what was going on, and I left in a hurry. I guess it was stupid to go in the first place, but I thought it would be a good way to meet some people." He directed an accusing look at Darcy. "No one asked me if I wanted to go to the dance."

Darcy concentrated on her hamburger. She wasn't about to acknowledge Megan's smug, know-it-all smile.

Back at school, Darcy and Mike walked together toward their classes. Tiffin ran up, shoved between them, and latched onto Mike. "Thank you for taking me home Friday night. You were a real lifesaver." She laid her head against his arm. "I'll have to think of a way to repay you."

Shock at Tiffin's appearance overrode Darcy's anger at her rude behavior. Today Tiffin had taken sleaze to a whole new level. The bottom half of her outfit perfectly suited the summer temperatures, which still soared in the mid-to-high nineties. Her chubby toes with chipped polish extended beyond the soles of her high-heeled sandals, and her tight, short shorts broke at least a dozen dress code rules. But on top she wore a long-sleeved tee. It would have been modest except for its revealing neckline. At least Tiffin's chest wouldn't be overheating.

What stunned Darcy more than Tiffin's outfit, though, was the news that Mike gave her a lift home. Everyone in school knew Tiffin belonged to Reese, and Reese guarded his possessions fiercely. If he got the impression Mike was trying to steal his property, he could be more dangerous than a rabid pit bull.

CHAPTER SEVEN

Mike's body hurt in places he didn't know existed before today's basketball practice. He dragged himself across the school parking lot to his pickup and tossed his backpack into the bed. Even his fingers hurt as he fumbled with the key in the lock.

Behind him he heard the roar of a hemi engine and turned to see a familiar black truck pull up and stop. The truck's spotless paint and chrome wheels gleamed in the afternoon sun. A tinted power window lowered with a hum, revealing Reese at the wheel. A boy Mike had never seen at school rode shotgun. In the back of the quad cab sat another passenger, but Mike couldn't see his face.

"Hey, Albright, that's some rig you got there," Reese said with a smirk.

"Glad you like it." Mike turned back to his pickup and opened the door. He climbed in, hoping Reese would drive away, but no such luck. The last thing Mike needed was a fight on school property. He rolled down his window. "Something I can do for you, Reese?"

Reese continued to inspect the pickup. "I don't think I've ever seen anything quite like it. What make and model is that?"

"Didn't know you were so interested in old trucks. But since you asked, it's a '57 Studebaker TranStar." He turned the key in the ignition and pumped the gas pedal. The old engine whined, sputtered, and died. He groaned inside but hid his irritation from his hecklers.

Reese let out a sarcastic whistle. "Hope that beater didn't set you back much. Sounds like it's about ready for a demolition derby."

Mike kept his words steady. "I appreciate your concern, but don't lose any sleep over it. It's on loan from a friend. And it gets me where I need to go—to school and back home."

25

"To school and back, huh?" Reese shoved his designer shades up on his forehead and stuck a toothpick in his mouth. "That's what I wanted to discuss with you. The detour you took last Friday night." He chewed on the toothpick. "You seem like a nice enough guy, Albright. The kind who wouldn't want to cause any trouble. So I figured you probably hadn't gotten the word."

"What word would that be?"

"Every guy in town knows Tiffin belongs to me. No dude messes with her unless I'm around or he has my permission. You're new, so this time I'm just gonna issue a friendly warning." Reese put his elbow on the rim of the window and stuck his head out. "Don't be taking any more detours with my girl."

Mike nodded. "You're right. I'm not the kind of guy who causes trouble." He leaned out of his own window. "But I'm not the kind who runs from it, either."

Reese sat silently, an expression of disbelief frozen on his face. After a while, he shrugged and spoke in a low snarl. "Suit yourself. It's your funeral." He gunned his engine a couple of times and tore across the parking lot.

Mike's pickup started after much cajoling and patient persistence. As he drove home, he steered with one hand and twisted a radio knob with the other. All he got was static.

Just as well, he thought, and switched the knob to *Off*. He hadn't found any stations which appealed to him since coming to Easton. The music in Oklahoma was a lot different from what he was used to.

He rested his head against the cab's back window and some of his tension dissolved. He'd enjoy the sounds of nature this afternoon—at least the sounds he could hear above the chugging and clattering of his pickup's motor. Maybe a leisurely drive home would diffuse some of his anger at Reese and his buddies.

The crest of a hill provided him with a panoramic view of the countryside. Fields of golden wheat, land plowed in even furrows, and cattle grazing in a rolling pasture gave evidence of the few remaining farms surrounding Easton. He was admiring the beautiful scenery when he spotted something not so beautiful. About a mile ahead, Reese's truck was parked on the right side of the road.

Mike's muscles tightened. He continued down the road at the same steady speed, but now he sat tensed, ready for any sudden maneuvers he might have to make.

When he passed the truck, he heard the roar of the engine. In his rear-view mirror, he saw gravel spewing behind the truck's back wheels. The tires hit the pavement with a screech, and the truck fish-tailed, leaving burned rubber marks on the road.

Baying and howling came from the cab of the truck. The growl of the engine grew louder. Reese and his buddies were closing in on him like a pack of hounds.

"Okay," he muttered. "Time to rodeo." He pressed on the accelerator and cut the steering wheel sharply to the right. The pickup— half rolling, half flying—took off across a vacant field. It threatened to self-destruct as it rattled and bucked over the rough terrain.

He had no idea where he was going, but up ahead he spied a thicket. If the pickup held together long enough, maybe he could hide there. He wasn't afraid of these Breadbasket bubbas. In his experience, he'd seen much worse. But if he could, he'd just as soon avoid a confrontation. For now, anyway.

Minutes later he sat behind a clump of trees and brush, turning the key and stomping the gas pedal. The engine gave no sign of life other than an occasional wheeze.

He opened the door and listened. The call of a mockingbird and the buzz of insects floated on the still, warm air. A cow mooed in the distance. He smiled at what he didn't hear. Reese must have decided not to follow. Probably didn't want to mess up his paint job.

"Sorry, fella," he said and patted the dash. "At least you went out with a fight."

He grabbed his backpack from the bed of the pickup and started walking. At the top of a rise, he paused. Shielding his eyes from the sun, he studied the huge rock formation that jutted from the ground in the distance. "Where in the world did that come from?"

He sprinted across the field to explore.

* * * *

"Mike! It's good to hear from you. I would ask you how it's going in Easton, but if you're contacting me, my guess is you're having problems."

Mike would never bother Col. Michael in the middle of a mission unless it was absolutely necessary. The episode this afternoon made it necessary. He recounted the experience with Reese and expressed no hope of things improving without some kind of intervention.

"No doubt about it, these guys are trouble," the colonel said. He paused to think through the problem. "You know, of course, we could handle this easily if our force chose to employ conventional methods. However, as you also know, we never do that. We choose not to use coercion or extraordinary means, and we can do nothing which would alert others of our...shall we say...special capabilities."

Mike had heard this information many times. "Yes, sir, I realize that."

The colonel said nothing for a while. Then he spoke slowly, thinking out loud. "Perhaps we could...another agent...yes! I'm sure this will work! Don't worry another minute, Mike. Help is on its way."

"Thank you, sir. I appreciate that. It's been good talking to you."

"You did the right thing to contact me. Remember what I told you. You're not in this alone."

A sense of relief came over Mike. He had no idea in what form help would arrive, but he hoped it got there fast.

CHAPTER EIGHT

Darcy lifted her head to catch the breeze as she trudged across the school parking lot. This cool October weather brought a long-awaited break from the searing summer heat and re-charged most people's energy and enthusiasm. But it did little to improve her current frustration.

She mentally reviewed her "to do" list: school, tennis practice, homework, student council activities. Today, her one afternoon with no work or practice, she had stayed at school until almost 5:00 to plan decorations for the Harvest Moon Dance.

For the millionth time since school started, she considered dropping her armload of books and taking off—taking off to any place far away from school, responsibilities, and, most of all, Tiffin.

"Hey, Darcy, wait up!"

She craned her neck and squinted in the direction of the call, unsure of what she saw. Mike was pedaling toward her on a rusty, creaking bicycle that must have been at least fifty years old. He rolled up beside her and pressed on the brakes which complained with a loud squeal.

"Hi, Mike. Why are you still at school, and"—she couldn't hold in her laugh—"what in the world are you doing on that thing?"

"I've been at basketball practice and what do you mean 'that thing'?" He made a sweeping gesture. "This happens to be a 1959 Western Flyer with dual headlamps, whitewalls, taillight, and genuine *chrome* tank and fenders. It's a classic among bike collectors. Show a little respect, please."

"I'm terribly sorry," Darcy said. "But not being a bike collector, I had no idea it was such a prize."

"Well, now that you've been duly informed, I expect nothing but admiration whenever you see me riding it in the future. And if you show bona fide, eye-popping, jaw-dropping awe, I might give you a ride on the handlebars."

"I'll keep that in mind. But when you say, 'in the future,' how long into the future do you plan to be riding it? What happened to your pickup?"

His head dropped and he spoke with concern. "That's a sad story. Let's say what my pickup is suffering from isn't terminal, but the recovery period could be long and difficult. In the meantime, my landlady was kind enough to dig this out of her barn for me. For an indefinite period of time, it will be my main set of wheels."

Darcy resumed walking in the direction of her car. "I hate to dampen your enthusiasm about cruising around town on such an awesome vehicle, but you do know, don't you, we are officially in the fall season? In Oklahoma, fall can mean some nasty weather—nasty as in cold and wet. That fine Western Flyer might get a bit breezy."

Mike walked along with her, pushing the bike. "For your information, that happens to be the best feature about this bike. It gives me the perfect excuse to hitch rides with all the cute girls at school. And you might be the first one I ask."

Since the second week of school—the day they had driven to The Tasty Treat together—Mike and Darcy had become good friends. They talked and joked in homeroom, and Mike often walked her to her classes. He sometimes made flirtatious remarks such as the one he'd just made, but she didn't take them seriously. Judging from the way half the girls in school swooned over him, she suspected he said things like that to a lot of them.

Still, more and more, she found herself wishing he would ask her out. She wasn't looking for a serious romance—just something a little beyond the "friends" status. Today she decided to give the relationship a nudge.

"I'll tell you what," she said. "I won't make you ask. I'm completely bummed from school today and need an attitude adjustment. If you want to stow your bike in the back of my car, I'll give you a ride to MugShots for the caffeine fix of your choice. My treat."

"That's the best offer I've had all day." He flashed a satisfied grin. "See, this bike gimmick is working already."

CHAPTER NINE

With Darcy's assistance, Mike loaded his bike into the back of her Beetle convertible. The effort was like squeezing a size-10 foot into a size-6 shoe, but they finally managed. They crept toward the coffee shop with the bike's front wheel sticking out of the backseat, revolving and creaking in the wind.

"Not to sound full of myself," Darcy said, "but I do have a reputation for being kind of cool. You do realize, don't you, I'm now totally risking that?"

"Yeah, but I'm so-o-o worth it."

Keeping her eyes on the road, she shook her head.

Mike checked out the interior of the Beetle with an approving nod. "This car is definitely not designed for hauling anything larger than a book bag, but it's cool. How'd you get it?"

She told him how she had fallen in love with the little yellow car with its black ragtop the first time she saw it on the used car lot. "I've owned it almost two years now, and its color and cute shape still make me feel good just to look at it. The Sevens christened her Bee—short for Bumblebee. She's perfect for 'buzzing' around town."

Mike groaned loudly. "Your pun stinks," he said, "but I can't disagree with your choice of cars. It's a good fit for you."

"Well, my dad did plenty of disagreeing. He wanted me to buy some big, hulking SUV. Claimed it would be much safer and have plenty of room to haul my tennis equipment. But I couldn't picture myself in one of those gas-guzzling monstrosities." She raised her hand, palm up. "I mean, do I look like one of those off-the-beaten-path, blazing-new-trails types?"

He didn't know what one of those types was supposed to look

like, but he was pretty sure the right answer here was, "Not at all."

"Exactly. So what do I need with a car like that? Anyway, we finally compromised. Dad bought me Bee with two stipulations: I had to pay for insurance and gas, and I couldn't drive her on the highway."

Mike nodded again. "Sounds reasonable to me."

* * * *

At MugShots, Darcy saved a table on the patio while Mike waited for the drinks. She used this time to chill. To her, autumn was the most beautiful season in Easton. The daytime temperatures seldom rose beyond the seventies, and the sun shone a sunflower yellow in Wedgewood blue skies. In the evenings, those famous Oklahoma winds became gentle breezes, which required only a sweater or light jacket.

She observed the surroundings of the coffee shop. When the sun's rays caught them at this time of day, the leaves of the sugar maples glowed fluorescent red and orange. Mounds of yellow, gold, and maroon chrysanthemums provided splashes of color against outcroppings of sandstone. The peaceful, colorful scene allowed her to forget her earlier wish to be somewhere else.

"You look like you're a thousand miles away."

Darcy peered up to see Mike's disarming smile above two mugs of latte. The late afternoon sun formed a brilliant orange ball behind him. For a fleeting moment, the scene reminded her of a Renaissance painting of a saint, his head encircled by a halo. Then she blinked, and the ethereal image was gone.

A bit rattled, she reached for one of the mugs. "Actually, I haven't been so here in a long time."

"That's a strange thing to say. What do you mean 'so here'?"

She confided in him all she had been experiencing over the past few weeks—a longing to get away from Easton, to escape all the pressures of school. She didn't tell him Tiffin was a large part of her desire to leave.

"On the way to The Tasty Treat, you promised to fill me in on Easton, but then we forgot about it," he said. "How about now?"

She took a sip of her latte. "I'm embarrassed I don't know as much as I should. I've heard Easton used to be a sleepy little country town a few miles north of Oklahoma City. It's hard to picture it now, but it was mostly farms and ranches then. In the seventies, it exploded into a bustling suburb. Most of the people work in the city, but live and send

34

their kids to school here."

"What's the population?"

She twisted her mouth to one side. "I think, about 80,000."

"That's bigger than I thought."

She nodded. "It's bigger than most people think. But you can see it's a growing place. It has a lot of the advantages of a big city, but in some ways it still has a small-town feel. I mean, if we get bored, we can always go to a mall, or a movie, or a sports event, but then we still have places like The Tasty Treat. That place has been here since the fifties. My dad told me up until the eighties it was *the* hangout for kids. It's not nearly as popular now, but whenever I go there, I like to imagine how it used to be."

Mike folded his arms on the table and leaned forward. "What do you think it was like?"

She smiled dreamily. "Oh, you know. Everybody meeting after school for a snack, kids circling round and round to show off their cars or check out the action. Songs like 'Earth Angel' playing on their radios. Sometimes I wish life could be as uncomplicated as it was back then."

"Do you think it was that simple?"

"Probably not. I'm sure those kids had problems, too. But it's a nice idea." She sat up straight. "Anyway, I guess what we have now is good in its way. I mean, we do have five Starbucks and two Walmart Supercenters. Not bad for a place Hollywood depicts as full of oil wells and cowboys, huh?"

He gazed at her. "Not bad at all." Then he shifted in his chair and cleared his throat. "You said you wanted to get away. Right now you sound more like the president of the Chamber of Commerce than someone who's ready to hop the next freighter out of town."

She agreed she probably did. A little embarrassed, she couldn't believe how much of her personal life she had revealed to him. She seldom shared her deepest feelings—especially her problems—with anyone except Megan. But his relaxed manner and openness made it easy for her to let down her guard. "Gosh, I'm sorry. I usually don't talk nonstop. I hope I didn't bore you to tears."

"No way. I appreciate the civics lesson. And I'm glad you trust me enough to be so open with me. I mean, I'm practically a stranger to you."

This fact caught her by surprise. For some unknown reason, she felt she knew him much better than she did. Something about his relaxed manner and smile made her feel secure. Like he was an old friend. And now Darcy was surprised again to realize something about him made her feel all jittery inside.

"Tell me this," he said. "If you could go anywhere in the world right now, where would you go?"

She tilted her head and shut her eyes. "If I could be anywhere right now, I would be...mmm... in the Berkshires in Massachusetts. I know that doesn't sound very exotic, but I went there once with my family over fall break. The scenery was unbelievable, and this time of year puts me in the mood for mountains, autumn leaves, wood-burning fireplaces...

"This is today, though. Ask me again in two weeks, and I'll probably tell you some place entirely different." She rested her chin in her hand. "Beyond the farthest star'—I heard those words in a song. I like that idea. Sometimes it sounds like the perfect location."

"Yeah, it does." He spoke in a whisper and with a far-away look in his eyes.

Darcy glanced around the almost empty patio. Most of the people had gone home for their evening meal. She should be doing the same, but hated to leave.

"Now that you know my entire life history," she said, "tell me something about yours. I know you're not from around here, but you've never said where you're from."

The stunned look on his face suggested the question had caught him by surprise. "I'm from up North—no place you've ever heard of. And you'd never find it on a map."

"Do you miss it?"

"I miss it a lot. It's beautiful there."

Like a host on a talk show, she prodded for more information. "You mentioned a landlady. Don't you live with your family?"

He stared into his cup and swirled the remaining latte. "Not at the moment. It's just my dad and I, and work keeps us separated a lot of the time. This is one of those times." He placed the mug on the table. "I called Aunt Rosie a landlady, but she's more than that. She's a longtime friend of the family, and I'm staying with her for a while in a big farmhouse five miles out of town. She treats me like a grandson, but I still miss home."

"That's too bad. What does your dad do? Is he in the service?"

Again he hesitated. "Yeah, something like that."

His vague answers puzzled her, but she was tired of playing Twenty Questions. Maybe there were personal matters he wasn't allowed to discuss or maybe they were too painful. If he wanted her to know more, he would tell her.

She swallowed her last drop of coffee. "This has been great, hanging out and relaxing. I don't get to talk to my friends enough these days. I hate to end it, but if I'm not home in a few minutes, the warden—a-k-a Mom—will be filing a missing persons report on me." She reached for her purse. "Let's do this again."

"We'll for sure do it again." He stood and helped her with her chair. He followed her out of the restaurant to the parking lot. "I've been kind of lonely since I've moved here. Aunt Rosie is sweet, but she's in her seventies. I see kids at school all day and at basketball practice, but I haven't made any close friends yet. I hope I can count you as my first close friend in Easton."

She smiled at him but said nothing. She hoped to be his *very* close friend.

At her car, both of them painstakingly extracted the bike from the back seat.

"Can I help you put the top up?" he asked.

"No, thanks." She looked up at the sky. "It's a nice night. I'll leave it down."

Still reluctant to leave, she rested against her car door and faced him. "Since I was accused of not mentioning the last school party to you, I want to officially notify you of the Harvest Moon Dance coming up. It's on the Saturday before Thanksgiving, and there's always a big crowd. It's kind of corny, but it's also a lot of fun."

"Thanks for the heads up. I'll mark it on my calendar."

Okay, she thought, this is where you're supposed to say, "Since I'm new and still don't know a lot of people, why don't we go together?" But he obviously wasn't tuned in to this telepathic message.

"It's not a big date event," she said. "Most kids go with a bunch of their friends, and everybody dances with everybody. The Sevens will all be there. Why don't you come with me, and I'll introduce you to some new people?"

"Sounds like fun. Can't wait." He swung his leg over the bike and placed one foot on a pedal in preparation to leave. Then, as if on a second thought, he planted both feet on the ground. He reached over and lightly swept a lock of hair out of her face, letting his palm linger against her cheek. "See you in homeroom tomorrow," he said and gave her his heart-melting smile. He pedaled across the parking lot, the dilapidated bike clattering and creaking as he went.

* * * *

The huge sun formed a fiery half circle on the horizon. Mellow from his conversation with Darcy, Mike ditched his usual route home in favor of a longer, more scenic one. This one passed through Hammond Park, one hundred sixty acres of urban forest resting squarely in the middle of town. Baseball diamonds, soccer fields, picnic tables, and children's playgrounds lined the outer edges of the tract. An asphalt hiking/biking trail wound its way past these into the heart of the acreage, which remained in a natural wooded state. The cool evening temperature and the fading light had cleared the area of all activity except that of frantic squirrels gathering nuts for the approaching winter. The squirrels' chatter, the rustle of fallen leaves, and the bike's rattle provided the only sounds in the deserted park.

Enjoying such moments of solitude marked him as strange in the world of teens, where being alone in public suggested you were some kind of social leper. But being different was nothing new or particularly worrisome to him. He cleared his mind of history facts, calculus problems, coaches' instructions, student gossip and used this time for quiet meditation.

When he went around a curve, he saw only the dense brush and foliage which edged the trail. But his reverie was interrupted by angry shouting and crying.

CHAPTER TEN

"You're lyin'! What did I tell you I'd do if I ever caught you lyin' again?"

"Get your hands off me! You don't own me. I'm not your property!"

"You think not? Well, maybe you better think—"

Mike's squeaky brakes must have alerted the quarrelers of his approach. *Great.* If he ever took up espionage, he'd definitely need another set of wheels.

He rounded another turn and stopped. Reese and Tiffin stood in the middle of the path, Reese gripping Tiffin's shoulders in both hands. Their faces were flushed with anger. Tears streaked Tiffin's cheeks. The couple turned toward Mike, their startled round eyes reflecting the proverbial deer-in-the-headlights look. Reese released his grip on Tiffin and squared his body to confront Mike face to face. He held his muscular arms at his sides, flexed his biceps, and formed two tight fists.

Tiffin instantly assumed her beauty-pageant smile and ran over to Mike. "Mike, where did you come from?" Confusion replaced her cheerful act. "And why are you riding this?" she asked, pointing at the bike.

Mike began, "I had some difficulty—"

"Yeah, okay, this is all fascinatin'," Reese interrupted, "but Tiffin and I were in the middle of a conversation. Maybe you should toddle off on your kiddy toy there and let us finish it in private."

Tiffin faced Reese, her hands on her hips. "And maybe, Reese,"— she attacked the *s* with a snakelike hiss—"you shouldn't be so rude. As a matter of fact, this conversation *is* finished." She turned again to Mike, batted her eyelashes, and spoke in her little girl voice. "I haven't been on a bike since I was in fourth grade. Would you mind giving me a ride to my car in the parking lot?"

Mike was uneasy with the way Tiffin was coming on to him, but he wanted to get her out of what appeared to be a difficult—and maybe dangerous—predicament. "Sure. Hop on," he said. He helped Tiffin balance herself on the handlebars.

As they rolled past him, Reese grunted. "You can ride off into the sunset with your hero, Tiffin, but don't think this matter is over."

Tiffin raised her hand over her head and waved back at him. "See you', Reese. Bye-byeee." Her parting words trailed off as she made her escape.

Mike pushed down hard on the pedals to get away from Reese. The ride was wobbly at first but smoothed out as the bike picked up speed.

"Thanks for coming to my rescue," Tiffin said. "I guess you could tell that was *not* a friendly conversation we were having."

"Yeah, it sounded pretty heated." Mike chose his next words carefully. "I don't know Reese all that well, but from the times I've been around him, he seems kind of ...moody. One minute he's fine and the next he's ready to fight. Think you're safe with him?"

Tiffin spoke almost too quickly. "Oh, he's fine. He had a bad day. When he cools down, he'll call me and apologize and everything will be okay. He talks big sometimes, but he's a nice guy."

Mike wondered if she was trying to convince him or herself.

Tiffin leaned back and rested her head against Mike's chest. "It's sweet of you to be so concerned about me, though."

Mike didn't know exactly how to respond to this, so he continued to pedal and let Tiffin do all the talking—something she did with little effort.

When they reached the parking lot, Mike let Tiffin off at her car, an expensive, late-model SUV. On his first day of school, Mike noted an SUV was the vehicle of choice among the affluent students and those who wanted to appear affluent. He already knew in which of these categories Tiffin belonged.

"Are you sure you'll be okay?" Mike asked.

"Yeah, I'll be fine. I'll be long gone by the time Reese gets to his truck, and I'm going straight home. Like I said, he'll be all ready to make up before the night's over."

Tiffin climbed into her car but left the door open. A huge smile lit up her face. "You' know, it's funny. We have classes together, but we never talk much at school." She gave Mike's shoulder a squeeze and rested her hand there. "I'd love to get to know you better. Sometime if you want to go to a movie or hang out, give me a call."

"Yeah…well…" Mike fumbled for words and avoided any eye contact.

Tiffin's smile faded. She removed her hand and dug in her purse for her keys. "Reese likes to make people think he owns me, but there's nothing official between us. Her tone became defiant. "I know for a fact he plays around with other girls. No reason I can't have some fun of my own."

Tiffin put the key in the ignition and slammed the car door. Without giving Mike another glance, she stomped on the gas pedal and tore across the parking lot.

* * * *

Before Darcy left MugShots, she tried calling Megan. What had happened wasn't earth-shattering news, but Darcy still wanted to share it with her best friend. When she got no answer, Darcy remembered Megan met with drama club on Tuesday nights, so she texted her. *nd2tlk*

Darcy glanced at her watch then pulled out of the parking lot. She wished she could cruise around for a while, thinking of her conversation with Mike, remembering the feel of his hand against her cheek. But if she didn't get home right away, her parents would be conducting their own version of Twenty Questions. Darcy played her favorite song, "Inside Your Heaven," and sang along with Carrie Underwood as she drove toward her house on the edge of town.

The route home passed several acres of undeveloped woodlands which sheltered all species of wildlife. This evening, up ahead, a deer was feeding by the side of road. Darcy recalled her dad's warning. "Deer are plentiful in this area, so always be alert. If you see one, slow down and be ready to brake. Whatever you do, don't swerve to miss it…even if it jumps in front of you. Losing control of your car can be much more dangerous than hitting a deer."

Tonight Darcy followed her dad's instructions. She let up on the gas and poised her foot over the brake as she cruised past the deer. It turned away from the road and bounded into the thick woods.

After dinner, Darcy sat at her desk and tried to work but couldn't concentrate. Megan called and demanded to know everything. Darcy told her every detail of the conversation with Mike. "It's no big deal, but —"

"Are you kidding? It's bigger than big! It's ginormous! I'm telling you, girl, that guy is totally into you. I mean, *totally*. I could tell from the very first day of school."

Not limiting her cheerleading to games and pep assemblies, Megan sometimes went a little overboard in support of her friends. But tonight Darcy let Megan ramble on. She needed all the encouragement she could get.

Darcy finished her homework and crawled into bed. Her conversation with Mike kept replaying in her brain. She wanted to stay awake and think about Mike's arms around her at the upcoming dance, but sleep overtook her.

* * * *

Tiffin lay in her bed thumbing through a *People* magazine while a music video played on the TV. When her cell phone rang, she checked the caller's name and swore.

"What do you want?" she snapped.

"Hey, babe. Want to grab something to eat?" Reese talked as if nothing had happened earlier.

"No."

"Come on, Tiffie. Don't be that way. You're not still mad about the park, are you?"

"You scared me. I don't like to be threatened."

"Aw, I didn't mean it. You know I'd never hurt you." Reese talked like a parent pacifying an upset child. "You know you're my favorite girl. Don't I take good care of you?"

Tiffin softened a little. She always gave in to him. The fights frightened her, but when they were over, Reese could be very generous.

"No, I'm not still mad, I'm just tired." She faked a huge yawn. "I'll see you tomorrow."

"I'll be dreaming of you all night long," Reese murmured. "You have sweet dreams, too."

"I will," Tiffin said and hung up.

She hadn't lied. She planned on having fantastic dreams. But they sure wouldn't be about Reese.

Tiffin turned off the TV and rolled over in bed. She was going to start on those sweet dreams right now. On a television talk show, they said people dream about whatever they're thinking when they drift off to sleep. She closed her eyes and thought about a bike ride through the park with a gorgeous guy—a guy with a mop of sandy hair, gentle brown eyes, and a smile to kill for.

CHAPTER ELEVEN

Darcy's eyes popped open and she sprang out of bed. This was the first morning since school started she had begun the day not wishing to be somewhere else. And this morning she would put some thought into what she wore. The concept of an occasional dress-up day wasn't foreign to her, but this year there hadn't been any point. Until today.

Her limited wardrobe presented a problem. It didn't take long to decide on some skinny-legged black jeans, but what to put with them? She stared at her hopeless tee shirt collection. Bor-ing.

About to trash the dress-up idea, Darcy had a flash of brilliance. Most of her mother's clothes Darcy wouldn't be caught dead in, but once in a while Carol Dunn displayed surprising fashion savvy. In her mother's closet, Darcy found a charcoal, mid-thigh cardigan which she belted over a plum tank top. Then she spied a pair of black suede, peep-toe pumps. Her mother wouldn't mind if she borrowed them just for today.

Darcy liked the sophisticated image she saw in the mirror. But something was missing. She ran back to her own room and rummaged through her jewelry box. Silver hoop earrings the size of saucers added the perfect touch.

Today, instead of a convenient ponytail, Darcy decided to go with big hair. She dug out her curling iron and formed loose, soft waves around her face. She carefully applied her make-up and even took the time to curl her eyelashes. After smearing on a coat of sheer pink gloss, she checked in the mirror and practiced her most enchanting smile.

When Darcy walked into the kitchen, her mother's look of surprise turned to approval. "I like that outfit." Carol stirred her coffee and studied the clothes a moment longer. Then she frowned. "I should.

Most of it's mine."

"Do you mind?" Darcy asked sheepishly.

Carol smiled. "No, but next time you might ask first. And be sure you return everything to my closet." She emptied the last of her coffee into the sink and rinsed the cup. "It's good to see you taking an interest in your appearance. Since school started, all I've seen you in are jeans and tee shirts. Why the sudden change?"

Darcy shrugged. "The weather?"

Carol started out the door but stopped and gave Darcy a sly grin. "I'll be sure and thank the weatherman."

That morning, getting dressed had kept Darcy so occupied she hadn't been nervous. Now, as she walked toward homeroom, her stomach tossed and pitched like a plane in a thunderstorm. Maybe she had made way too much of what happened the evening before.

Megan joined Darcy in the hallway. "Hey, Dars, you are stylin' today. Love your hair." She scrutinized Darcy's face. "And how do you do your eyes like that?"

"Thanks. You don't think this is too over-the-top for school, do you?" Megan did more for a girl's ego than an air-brushed Glamour Shot.

"No way. You should dress like this every day. Wait. Forget I said that. If you looked like this every day, the rest of us girls wouldn't stand a chance."

Darcy took into consideration Megan had shifted into her cheerleading mode. But at least she had temporarily stilled the turbulence in Darcy's stomach.

In homeroom, Mike smiled at Darcy and indicated he had saved her the desk next to his. She sat down, and for the full twenty minutes of homeroom, they talked as easily as they had last night at MugShots. The dismissal bell rang, and Mike and Darcy rose to leave.

"I'd ask you to lunch," Mike said, "but you already know my transportation problem. I'm doomed to spend lunchtime in that dungeon deceptively labeled *school_cafeteria*." He followed Darcy to the door. "You could join me there. I hear the dungeon crew does wonders with dragon meat."

Darcy scrunched up her nose. "I'm pretty sure I'm allergic to dragon meat. Why don't Bee and I save you from certain torture and take you to lunch?"

"Good idea. Glad you thought of it. Are you meeting the Sevens?"

"Not today. Everyone has other plans. So you're the one rescuing me from a lonely lunch break."

"Always glad to come to the aid of a maiden in distress." Mike executed a courtly bow, then walked with Darcy to a hallway intersection. "Why don't I wait for you by the doorway to the senior parking lot?" he asked before they went their separate ways. "Maybe we can beat the mass-exit hysteria."

"Sounds good. See you then."

Darcy stopped by her locker before going to her next class. She opened it and found an advertisement for Slim-Fast® taped to the inside of the door. It didn't take Darcy long to figure out who put it there. The implied message infuriated Darcy, but she was more upset Tiffin had learned her combination. This prank was one of Tiffin's milder ones. What would Darcy find in her locker next time?

In fourth hour, Darcy checked the time: *11:42*. She scribbled some doodles in the margins of her literature notes, then glanced at her watch again: *11:43*. The time was passing slower than a turtle on Valium. She hoped she wouldn't be tested on anything her teacher said today because she hadn't heard a word. Her thoughts kept ping-ponging between how much she liked Mike and how much she despised Tiffin.

At last the bell rang, and Darcy raced down the hallway to get ahead of the lunch traffic. She saw Mike standing at the appointed exit, but he was talking to some— *Aghhh!* Tiffin again. She was looking up at Mike with her star-struck gaze, and, of course, she was groping him.

Apparently Darcy wasn't the only one today who had dressed to impress. Tiffin wore a green tee shirt, stretched to its bursting point. Below it a black spandex mini-skirt hugged her ample rear like a second skin.

"Hey, Darcy!" When Tiffin saw her, she greeted Darcy like an old friend. "I was telling Mike how much fun I had last night."

"Doing what? Cutting out weight-loss ads?"

Tiffin's face was the picture of innocence. "I don't know what you mean. I was talking about meeting Mike in the park." She looked up at him again. "You should get him to take you for a ride on his bike sometime. The park is so-o-o romantic in the dark." Tiffin turned back to Darcy, cheerful and friendly. "Call me. Let's do lunch."

Darcy knew this act was all for Mike's benefit. There was as much chance of the two of them "doing lunch" as there was of Darcy asking Tiffin for fashion advice.

"By the way, Darcy," Tiffin said, "love your outfit. It's so slenderizing. Can you believe we used to call you Dumpy Darcy?" Tiffin held up her hand, palm facing forward, and flicked her fingers up and down. "Bye," she said and walked away.

Tiffin spoiled their plans for a fast getaway, so Darcy and Mike saved time by grabbing sandwiches and drinks at a convenience store. At a picnic table in the park, Darcy seethed as the scene with Tiffin replayed in her mind.

"Ground control to Darcy. Please give your location."

Jarred from her thoughts, Darcy snapped, "How about you give yours."

"Excuse me?"

"How about you give your location? Last night. What was that about seeing Tiffin in the park? You must get around pretty fast on that bike." The words slipped out before Darcy could stop herself, and she immediately regretted them. She looked across the table at Mike, expecting to see anger. Instead, she saw concern.

"Is that why you're upset?" he asked.

Her eyes tracked an ant making its way across the table. "I'm sorry. That was mean and so none of my business. You don't owe me any explanations about where you go or who you see."

"I'm sorry, too."

Her head jerked up. Mike's response was not what she expected and made her feel guiltier.

"I should've explained right away," he said.

She started to protest, but he insisted. "Believe me. Tiffin was making a lot bigger deal out of it than it was. I was riding my bike through Hammond Park and saw Tiffin and Reese having an argument. Tiffin seemed upset, so I gave her a ride to her car." He chuckled. "All that about the park being 'so-o-o romantic' must have been with someone before I got there."

Darcy ducked her chin, now too ashamed to face Mike. "I believe you. I've had some experience myself with Tiffin's overactive imagination. You'd think by now I'd learn not to listen to anything she says. But we have a history, and it's not pretty. It's hard to ignore a lot of what she says and does."

"Want to talk about it?"

Darcy thought for a moment, not sure how much to tell Mike. She didn't want to sound like a whiner. Maybe if she gave him a little background, though, she could justify her earlier outburst.

She began with the first day she met Tiffin. "My family and I had moved across town, and I had to go to a new middle school. I was upset at first, but I decided to make the best of it. The weekend before I started there, I bought some new jeans and a cool tee shirt at the mall. I spent every last penny I'd been saving for months."

"Why?"

Of course, he would ask that. Only a girl would understand how the right clothes can give the confidence needed on the first day at a new school. Darcy tried to explain but was sure the whole concept was lost on a guy whose personal style could best be described as *clean*.

"Anyway," she continued, "I walked into my new homeroom and saw a circle of girls standing around talking. They were all giggling, and I heard stuff like 'Tiffin, tell us…,' 'Tiffin, show me…,' 'Tiffin, where did….' I took a deep breath and went over and introduced myself."

Darcy swallowed hard to choke back the lump forming in her throat. The memory of the event still caused pain.

"Only one girl bothered to acknowledge me. A girl with curly red hair and braces said 'Hi,' but she didn't look at me. She kept her eyes glued on the center of the circle. I stood there like a big dummy, wondering what to do next. Then I heard a Mickey Mouse voice ask, 'Who's that?' "

Darcy recalled the first time she laid eyes on Tiffin. She didn't bother to describe it to Mike, but that first image of Tiffin would haunt her forever. Tiffin wore a flouncy, ruffled skirt which barely covered her behind and a skin-tight, hot-pink tee with the words *Naughty but Nice* spelled out in rhinestones across the chest. Bleached-blond hair, sparkly hoop earrings, and caked-on make-up completed Tiffin's hooker-in-training ensemble.

"Tiffin stood there staring at me for what seemed like years," Darcy said. "Then she turned to the girl next to her. 'I think that's the outfit I gave to Goodwill,' she said as loud as she could. She broke into her hyena laugh, and right on cue, her little wannabes joined in.

"And that was my introduction to Tiffin. Her comment about my clothes was just the beginning. From that point on, Tiffin's main goal in life was to make mine miserable. And she pursued it with the same passion she devotes to shopping and partying."

Darcy sat with her shoulders slumped. Then she pulled them back and sat up straight. "I'm sorry. I sound like some tragic soap opera queen. But I didn't want my earlier reaction to Tiffin make you think I'm a complete witch."

Mike reached across the table and placed his hand on Darcy's arm. "Nothing you could ever do or say would make me think that."

"Oh, yeah? You might change your mind when you hear what I have to say now." Darcy did her best Wicked Witch of the North impersonation. "We have to get back to school, my pretty."

"Can I call you tonight?" Mike asked on the ride back to school.

"Sure. You don't have to ask permission, you know."

He gave her an embarrassed grin. "Yeah, I know. But I have basketball practice after school and an essay to write for history, so it'll be kind of late. Is that okay?"

"That's fine. I've got a lot of homework, too. I'll be up."

At school, Darcy found Megan in the hallway and told her about lunch. "Maybe my outburst over Tiffin wasn't such a disaster after all. For the first time since school started, Mike's going to call me."

That afternoon, Darcy found a deep scratch, stretching from the front to the rear bumper on the driver's side of her car.

CHAPTER TWELVE

At The Market Basket, Mike stood in the checkout line with Aunt Rosie and helped the checker bag groceries. He glanced out of the store's plate glass window and saw Reese and his two partners in crime. They were eyeing his bike which was propped against a No Parking sign. Whatever they were up to couldn't be good.

"Mike, dear, I'll take these two bags and go ahead to the car," Aunt Rosie said. "You bring the rest of the groceries when they're sacked."

Mike watched her shuffle out of the store, a grocery bag in each arm. But when she got outside, instead of going straight to her car, she approached Reese and his friends.

"What is she up to?" Mike muttered. He figured he'd better keep his eye on this situation. He saw her smile sweetly as she talked to the boys, and he saw the confusion on their faces. Then Mike shook his head in disbelief as she thrust her parcels into the arms of the two unidentified boys and they followed her across the parking lot. More surprising, Reese trudged behind them, fuming and pushing the rickety bike.

Mike grabbed the remaining sacks and rushed out the door.

"Oh, sweetie, look who I ran into," Aunt Rosie said when Mike caught up with them. She spoke as if she were introducing members of a Sunday school class. "Reese says he knows you from school, but these other young men are Lance and Tucker."

Mike gave a quick *hey*, and the threesome responded only with upward jerks of their chins.

Aunt Rosie dabbed at her face with a lace hankie. "I saw these gentlemen admiring your bike so I thought they must be friends of yours. I explained to them you met me here after basketball practice to help with the shopping, and they insisted on helping, too." She stuffed the hankie in her purse. "It's so refreshing to meet polite young people these days."

She led her entourage to an ancient sedan which was slightly shorter than a bus. While Mike placed his sacks in the back seat of the car, she rooted through her purse again. "Oh, here they are," she said at last. She jiggled a set of keys in front of the boys' faces and then unlocked the lid to the cavernous trunk.

"Now, Mr. Reese," she said. "If you'll put the bike in here at an angle, I believe the rest of the groceries will fit nicely."

With zombie-like movements, the boys loaded the bike and groceries according to her instructions. When they finished, she started to close the lid but stopped abruptly.

"Oh, where are my manners?" she scolded herself. "I'm sorry I don't have any change on me, but I believe you fellows deserve a fitting reward." She reached into one of the grocery bags and opened a box. Then she thrust something into the hands of each of the semi-comatose boys.

When Mike saw the "fitting reward," he slid into the driver's seat of the car. He wanted to be ready in case the two of them had to make a fast getaway.

Aunt Rosie slammed the lid, toddled to the passenger side of the car, and got in. She handed him the keys, and he wasted no time in making their departure.

Leaving the parking lot, he glanced back at Reese, Lance, and Tucker who had recovered their senses. Reese looked at the contents of his hand, swore, and flung the package to the ground. But Lance and Tucker grinned with childish delight at the prizes in their hands. Each boy eagerly tore into his package of Ding Dongs.

* * * *

Darcy was battling a calculus problem and losing when her cell phone blared "Boomer Sooner," the University of Oklahoma fight song. She checked the caller's name, and as she hoped, it was Mike. She let the song play a few seconds before answering.

"Hello."

"Hey, Darcy, it's me like I promised. Hope it's not too late."

"No, it's fine. My parents don't care how late I stay up as long as I don't disturb them or my grades don't slip."

"I would've called earlier, but I just finished my homework. Is there anything you want to know about the SALT II treaty during the Carter administration? I'm an expert on the subject now."

She didn't have to think about it. "That would be a negative."

"Good. We can get right to the point. Today at lunch you said Tiffin's goal in life was to make yours miserable. What else has she done?"

"Are you sure you want to hear this? It's a long story."

"I've got all night."

"Okay, but remember, you asked."

She moved from her desk to her bed and plumped up the pillows before resting against them. This would take a while. Might as well get comfortable. Rufus jumped up on the bed beside her, and she stroked his head as she considered how much to tell Mike.

She hardly knew where to begin, but finally decided to start with the worst. The day Tiffin's bullying turned deadly. As she launched into her explanation, the details were as clear in her mind as the day they happened.

"After that horrible first day of school," she said, "I ran from Tiffin for the next two weeks. Every day I'd dash from classroom to classroom so I wouldn't be caught by her and her pack of she-wolves in the halls. At lunch, I hid out in the library, and I didn't even consider going into the girls' bathroom."

"Man, that's rough," Mike said.

"Tell me about it." Darcy's anger rose as she thought of those lonely, frightful days. "Besides the library, the only place in the whole school I felt safe was the hallway to the bus loop. Tiffin and her gang were way too cool to ride the bus. But one afternoon, they stormed into that hallway, laughing and yelling in their usual effort to attract attention."

"I get the picture," Mike said.

"I tried to make myself invisible by ducking down behind a group of students," Darcy said. "But Tiffin found me. I think she had a sixth sense for tracking me down. When she saw me, she screamed, 'Hey, Dump...I mean, Darcy.' Then she squeaked, 'Ha! That's good—Dumpy Darcy!' She and all her evil little toadies began chanting, 'Dumpy Darcy! Dumpy Darcy!'"

"Geez," Mike said. "I didn't know girls that young could be so mean."

"Are you kidding?!" Darcy shouted. Then she lowered her voice. "Sorry. But what planet are you from? Middle school girls can be the cruelest creatures on the face of the earth. The government should recruit them to combat terrorists." She said this as a joke—well, mostly as a joke —but then she grew serious.

She drew a deep breath before continuing. "I don't know what came over me, but all of the sudden, I'd had enough. I was tired of running and hiding. I turned to Tiffin and told her to shut up and stay away from me. At first Tiffin's eyes grew wide like she couldn't believe I'd actually stood up to her. Then a nasty grin formed on her face and she pushed her nose into a pig-like snout and started grunting and oinking." Darcy shuddered as the hideous sounds again formed in her memory. "When I turned and walked away, she and her wannabes trailed me, imitating Tiffin's pig sounds, growing louder and louder. I pushed my way through the students and managed to lose all my stalkers except Tiffin. When I finally reached the exit, she was still right on my heels. I charged through the double doors to the bus turnaround and felt a shove from behind."

Darcy paused. This was where the details became fuzzy. "What happened next is kind of a blur," she said. "You know, like one of those slow-mo scenes in a movie or a nightmare. I heard a horn and brakes squealing. And someone shouted, 'Watch out!' Then I saw a school bus coming right at me."

CHAPTER THIRTEEN

A low whistle pierced Darcy's ear. "Wow," Mike said with a hush. "No wonder it seems like a nightmare. It was. You're lucky to be alive."

Darcy explained that before she had time to be frightened, a hand jerked her to safety. "I heard a calm voice say, 'You'd better be careful, dear. I don't think you're any match for a bus.'"

"Thank God someone was there," Mike said. "Who was it?"

"To this day, I have no clue. The whole thing was so surreal. The old lady had silver-white hair and a wrinkled but sweet face. I'd never seen her at school before… thought maybe she worked in the cafeteria or was a sub. She didn't yell at me for being stupid or insist on filing some kind of report."

"Did you ever see her again?"

"She asked me if I was okay and walked away. I never saw her again."

"Spooky."

"Yeah," Darcy agreed, "it's a little freaky. But she saved my life. I always call her my guardian angel. When you said, 'Thank God,' you were right. I don't know how you feel about this sort of thing, but as far as I'm concerned, she was a miracle from God."

"Umm…I'm okay with that," Mike said. "What about Tiffin? Any miracles there?"

"Not with Tiffin. Kind of with the Dumpy Darcy problem, though. Toward the middle of sixth grade, I started growing." She laughed. "*Up* not out. And I worked non-stop on my tennis game. By the time school started the next fall, I was tall and slim. My new appearance and abilities gave me more self-confidence. And, in spite of Tiffin's efforts, I'd acquired some new friends. So for the remainder of middle school, Tiffin had to look for other ways to torment me."

"I'm almost afraid to ask what she did."

"Oh, most of it was lame. I'd find hateful notes taped to my locker, insults and threats chalked on my driveway and sidewalk, lies of what a slut I was broadcast to Tiffin's 892 closest friends on Facebook. But no one who knew me believed them."

"Did Tiffin ever back off?"

"Not in middle school. But she did in high school."

"Did she grow up?"

Darcy scoffed. "Uh, no. Tiffin didn't mature—not emotionally, anyway. But she had to learn some new skills to survive in high school. She smiles and waves and pretends to be nice, but she doesn't fool many people. Everyone except members of her little clique is fed up with her. And even they make fun of her when she isn't around."

"Maybe she hasn't learned survival skills as well as you think."

Was that compassion in Mike's voice? Was he defending Tiffin? This was not the reaction Darcy expected. She liked the fact that Mike was nice, but sometimes that niceness could go too far. "I wouldn't worry about Tiffin if I were you," she said hotly. Then, feeling guilty about another outburst, she backed off. "You probably think I should get past all this, and believe me, I've tried." She paused and then spoke softly. "But it's a lot to get past." Her sigh grew into a yawn.

"I'm sorry," Mike said. "It's late. We both need to get some sleep. See you tomorrow?"

"Sure."

Instead of sleeping, Darcy tossed and turned. She had never told anyone about the bus incident until tonight. In talking about it, she realized her body had survived Tiffin's terror, but her spirit had sustained a crippling injury—an injury from which she had never fully recovered. She decided the only way to deal with her fears was to face them. The time had come to take care of Tiffin.

CHAPTER FOURTEEN

Over the next two days, Darcy considered ways to deal with Tiffin. She also considered another rule of tennis: Respect your opponent.

For whatever reason, Tiffin enjoyed playing the part of airhead. Maybe it got her a lot of attention, or maybe she thought boys liked girls who were dumb. Tiffin made no secret of her lousy grades, and whenever she was called on in class, she gave stupid answers that made everyone laugh.

But Tiffin was not the dummy she pretended to be. No one could be that clueless and be so manipulative at the same time. Tiffin was a force to be reckoned with all right. She was dishonest, conniving, and smart. And she would stop at nothing to get what she wanted.

But Darcy was smart and tenacious, also. And she had friends who would help her. Darcy sat at lunch with the Sevens on Friday and told them of her decision.

"Megan told me six years was long enough," Darcy said. "She was wrong." She cut off Megan's attempt to argue. "Six years is too long."

The Sevens broke out in cheers and high-fived Darcy and each other.

"So this is the plan," Darcy said when everyone quieted down. The Sevens leaned in to listen, as serious as secret agents planning a covert operation.

"I can't be watching Tiffin 24/7, but I think with a little networking, we can cover her at the times and places she's likely to do the most damage."

The Sevens nodded.

"We spread out before and after school and in between classes." Darcy held up her phone. "If one of us sees Tiffin in the area around my locker or my car, they text or call the rest of us. Whoever is closest to the area can notify the others the situation is covered."

"What about Reese?" Chad asked. "Think he's in on any of this with Tiffin?"

Darcy shook her head. "If he is, I think it's only as an advisor."

"Just the same," Chris said, "we better keep an eye on him, too."

"I like this plan," Megan said. A devilish grin spread across her face.

The following Tuesday, a chance to test the plan occurred. Darcy was walking to homeroom before school when her phone buzzed.

"Tiffin is lurking around your locker. I'm sure she's up to something," Megan said. "Do you want me to take care of this?" She asked the question with maybe a little too much enthusiasm.

"No, I've got it covered." Darcy altered her route and headed in direction of her locker. This was one encounter with Tiffin she was looking forward to.

"Need something, Tiffin?" Darcy asked.

Tiffin slammed the metal door. Her face reddened as she turned to face Darcy, and she shoved a brown paper bag behind her back.

"What's in the sack?" Darcy folded her arms across her chest. "Planting something in my locker? Booze? A joint? A rattlesnake?"

"You don't know what you're talking about," Tiffin sneered. "And you can't prove anything."

Darcy held up her phone with a picture of Tiffin holding onto the open locker door. "Think this would be proof enough? I'm not as vicious as you, so I won't post it on Facebook. Not yet. But the administration might find it interesting. Especially when I tell them I didn't give you my combination or permission to open my locker."

"They won't believe you."

"*Pff.* Given our past experiences with administrators, I'll take my chances." Darcy lowered her phone and locked her eyes on Tiffin's. "This time I'm letting you off the hook. But I'm changing my combination. If I find out you have the new one, I'm going straight to school security. And this picture will be all over the internet with an explanation of why you were suspended."

Tiffin drew her mouth into an angry pout. She stood in place, shifting her weight from foot to foot. Then, without another word, she huffed and prissed away.

On the way to homeroom, Darcy's heart was lighter than it had been in six years. She was almost giddy with her sense of power as she recalled the defeated expression on Tiffin's face. Or had it been fear? Darcy's euphoria faded. Her thrill of victory had had the lasting effect of a sixty-second carnival ride.

CHAPTER FIFTEEN

Adrenaline rushed through Mike' body, making sitting still impossible. This was the first Friday in November, and tonight's opening game against Braxton High would set the tone for the entire basketball season. Braxton, Easton's hated cross-town rival, had beaten the Eagles three years running, but this year held the hope of an Easton victory. Much of that hope rested on Mike.

Along with his excitement there was also a feeling of foreboding. Through experience he'd learned events like tonight's game often led to altercations off the court as well as on. Emotions ran high when bitter rivals clashed, and sometimes fans became aggressive. This possibility caused Mike more concern than the game did.

While Darcy chatted to him in homeroom, Mike drummed his fingers on the desk. Underneath it, his knee jiggled up and down. When Darcy paused in her conversation, Mike inserted a generic, "Cool."

Darcy frowned. "Did you hear anything I said?"

"Mmm…yeah, sure. Why?"

"I told you I think I bombed my calculus quiz yesterday, and you said, 'Cool.'" She laughed and placed her hand over his to still the drumming. "Are you worried about the game tonight?"

"Yeah, I can't quit thinking about it." Mike would let her believe he was worried about winning the game. It was hard to explain the out-of-control fan problem.

Darcy gave his hand a squeeze before she released it. "I know how you feel. Before a big tennis tournament, I can't eat, sleep, or think about anything else. Don't worry. The talk around school says you're the next Michael Jordan. Once you get over your pre-game jitters, you'll be fine." She gave him an encouraging smile. "And I can't wait to see you in action."

At lunch Mike joined Darcy and the Sevens at Taco Grande but ate hardly anything.

Chris tried to boost his confidence. "Mike, after the win tonight, why don't you come celebrate with us at Mario's Pizza? We'll have, like...a victory party. I'm sure Bee would be happy to give you a lift." Chris glanced at Darcy, who responded with an embarrassed grin.

"Thanks," Mike said," but I'll probably go straight home and collapse into bed. After games I'm drained. I doubt I'd be much fun. Probably fall asleep face down in the pizza."

Everyone agreed that would actually be a lot of fun to watch.

Back at school Cliff caught up with Mike in the hall. "Hey, good luck tonight. And don't sweat it. This game's going to be a blowout."

"Thanks."

"Also, I wanted to tell you we're planning a surprise birthday party for Darcy at Mario's after the game. I know you said you're too tired to go anywhere after a game, but if you can stop by for a little while, that'd be great."

"Thanks for telling me. I'll definitely be there."

Man, I'm such a jerk! Mike remembered now Darcy had mentioned she had a birthday coming up. She hadn't made a big deal of it— just said something about looking forward to turning eighteen.

He couldn't believe he'd forgotten. The game tonight had dominated his thoughts, and now there wasn't time to buy Darcy a gift. Well, he'd think of some way to make it up to her. He could start by winning this game.

In spite of the Sevens' efforts to calm his nerves, Mike spent the rest of the day worrying. It was not until the pre-game warm-up that he started to relax. When the coach called the team to the bench for a last-minute pep talk, Mike heard for the first time the chants and cheers coming from the packed bleachers. He scanned the crowd and spotted Darcy. She was sitting with all of the Sevens except Megan, who was on the gym floor in her cheerleader uniform, jumping around like a human pogo stick.

When Mike caught her eye, Darcy cupped her hands around her mouth. "Go, Mike!" she shouted and grinned. That was all the inspiration he needed. When the players took their positions for the opening toss, he was ready to do battle.

From the tip-off to the final buzzer, the game against Braxton was neck-and-neck, with every point hotly contested. Every time Easton scored, Braxton players answered it with two points of their own. But in the final mille-second, Mike stole the ball and, putting up a Hail Mary, bucketed it for the winning two points.

The teams barely had time to shake hands before the crazed Easton fans poured out of the stands. They swarmed the players, hugging and congratulating them. Mike looked through the crush of people for Darcy. He wanted to share this moment with her. But before he could find her, the coach called the players into the locker room.

After the coach's re-cap of the game and a hot shower, Mike left to join the others at Mario's. He walked through the now dimly-lit gym, empty except for a few custodians. He shuddered at the eerie, oppressive atmosphere. In a matter of a few minutes, the gym had gone from a place teeming with vitality to a gloomy, hollow pit. Mike started for the exit, but then remembered he needed a book from his locker.

Over the echoes of his footsteps in a deserted hallway, Mike heard a thud and the rattle of metal. He ran down the hall and turned the corner to experience déjà vu.

CHAPTER SIXTEEN

Mike could barely control his rage as he took in the scene before him. Tiffin was on the floor, cowering against a locker. The contents of her purse—make-up, keys, wallet, cigarettes—lay strewn across the floor. Reese loomed over her.

On seeing Mike, Reese cursed and shook his head. "Albright, did anyone ever tell you that you have lousy timing?" He walked toward Mike and stopped about three inches in front of him. "It seems to me," he said, pulling himself up to his full 5'6", "you're always interrupting serious talks between me and my girl."

"And it seems to me," Mike said between clenched teeth, "this 'talk,' as you call it, has become way too serious." He stepped around Reese as if he were no more a threat than a yapping terrier and knelt beside Tiffin. "Are you okay?"

Tiffin whimpered as she rubbed her hand against the back of her neck.

"Do you have your car here?" Mike asked.

Tiffin winced and nodded.

"You look pretty shaken. Why don't I load my bike into the back of your car and drive you home?" Mike gathered Tiffin's scattered belongings, helped her up, and directed her toward the exit.

Reese stood tense and motionless. "Just wait, you meddling, self-righteous prig," he shouted to Mike's back. "You're the big man now, but you might find it's not fun to tangle with the devil."

In Tiffin's SUV, Mike glanced at her as she leaned against - the passenger door , head bowed and tears trickling down her cheek.

He spoke to her in a caring but firm voice. "You know, this relationship you have with Reese might not be such a good thing for you.

I'm no expert, but everyone knows dating violence increases when steroids are involved."

Tiffin kept her head down and sniffed. "It's not what you think." She rubbed her nose with the back of her hand. "And besides, whoever said Reese uses steroids?"

In his frustration, Mike considered saying nothing, but he had to try at least once more. "Okay, believe what you want. Keep in mind, though, your face isn't going to be nearly as cute with missing teeth or a scar or a broken nose. And that's if you're lucky."

When there was no response from Tiffin, they rode in silence to her house. Mike pulled into the driveway and turned off the car engine. Again they sat in silence.

"I can take you home," Tiffin said finally.

"No, that's okay. You should go in and have your mom look at your neck. She might need to take you to the emergency room."

Mike opened the door and stepped to the rear of the car to unload his bike. He was looking forward to the long, quiet ride home. It would be a chance to collect his thoughts, get his anger toward Reese under control. "If your neck still hurts in the morning, be sure to see a doctor," he said. Any more warnings would be wasted.

"Yeah, I will. Thanks." Tiffin eased herself from the car and walked toward her house with her head hanging and her shoulders slumped. Her purse dangled at the end of her limp arm.

Mike knew this wasn't an act. Tiffin really was hurt. He knew because of the way she had gingerly stepped from the car. He also knew because she hadn't made a single pass at him all night.

* * * *

Junk mail, bills, and late notices cluttered the table in the entry way of Tiffin's house. The only light came from the television in the family room. *Family room*, thought Tiffin. That's a joke. As far as she knew, no family had ever lived here. She walked into the room where her mother reclined on the sofa, watching *Desperate Housewives* and sipping a martini. A scruffy Yorkshire terrier lay curled up next to her.

"Hey, girlfriend." Doris raised her glass as if offering a toast. She kept her eyes glued to the TV. "Where you' been all night?"

Tiffin cleared some clothes and movie magazines from an easy chair and slumped into it. "Dodie,"—Doris didn't like to be called Mom—"we have to talk."

"Can't it wait a few more minutes? This episode is almost over." Doris reached for an emery board on the coffee table and began filing her nails.

Tiffin slapped the arms of the chair with both hands and jerked up straight. "No, it cannot wait! Geez!"

Doris stopped her filing. "Get outta the way, Punkin."

The little dog growled when Doris shoved her off the couch. Doris grumbled a curse word, grabbed the remote, and punched the *Off* button. She switched on a lamp and shifted into her mothering mode. "Don't use that tone with me, missy, I—"

Doris stopped when she saw her daughter's rumpled clothes and mascara-stained face. She hurried over to Tiffin and squeezed beside her in the chair, suddenly the embodiment of motherly concern. "Oh, baby, what's wrong? Tell Dodie what happened." She put her arm around her daughter.

Tiffin rested her head on Doris's shoulder and held nothing back. Her shoulders heaved as years of pent up fear and worry found release. Doris continued holding her, patting her back, waiting until the crying subsided.

When it finally did, Doris released her hug and leaned away from Tiffin. "Okay, now. Tell me everything. Are there problems at school with a teacher? Are some of your friends being mean to you?" She grew feisty. "'Cause if they are, I'll take care of it in a hurry. I'll kick their—"

"Dodie! It's not school. Or other girls. It's Reese."

Alarm crossed Doris's face. "Did he break up with you?"

"No, but I wish he would."

Doris's smile reflected relief. She took Tiffin's hand in her own and patted it. "Oh, baby, you two are having a little lover's quarrel. You'll work it out."

Tiffin snatched her hand away. "Maybe I don't want to work it out."

"Of course, you do. Reese is a good catch. He might not be the most sensitive male on the planet, but he doesn't mean to hurt you. He buys you nice gifts. And his dad has plenty of money to provide for his son… and whoever his son marries." She added in a sing-song tone, "I'll bet there are tons of girls who wish they were in your place."

"I doubt it," mumbled Tiffin. "Anyway, I don't care about those things. Reese was nice enough when we started dating, but he keeps getting meaner and he's so controlling and jealous. Sometimes he scares me."

"*Hmph*. Tiffin, you were always such a drama queen." Doris reached for a cigarette, lit it, and inhaled deeply. She held the cigarette up between her index and middle fingers and raised her chin in the air. A thin line of smoke streamed from her mouth and nostrils. Then her raspy voice became cold and laced with resentment. "I hate to break this news to you, missy, but there are no perfect guys out there. And the sooner you learn that the happier you'll be." She took another drag on the cigarette. "Believe me. I should know."

Tiffin stood up and looked at her mother as if seeing her for the first time. Her chin began to quiver, and tears pooled in her eyes. "Don't you care what happens to me?"

"Oh, yeah, honey, I care. I care a lot. So let me give you some cold, hard facts." Doris's volume rose along with her irritation. "My current marriage status is *divorced*. I don't have a job and neither do you, so at the present there's no wage-earner in this family." She ground out her cigarette on a coaster. "In a few months, you turn eighteen, and if you don't go to college, that worthless dad of yours no longer owes me child support."

"Okay, so I'll go to college!"

Doris lit another cigarette. "Well, that sounds like a good plan, but the last time I checked, your grades didn't exactly indicate you were college material. So that doesn't leave us with a whole lot of options."

For all the sympathy she was getting, Tiffin might as well be talking to Punkin. She would never make her mother understand. She snatched her purse and stormed up the stairs.

But Doris wasn't through issuing motherly advice. She stood at the bottom of the stairs and yelled up. "Every relationship involves some give and take. If I were you, I'd re-think breaking up with Reese. He might not be perfect, but, like I said, perfect men don't exist."

Tiffin slammed the door to her bedroom. She trampled on the clothes that carpeted the floor and threw herself onto the unmade bed. Now, more than frightened or hurt, she was angry. She'd show her stupid mother. Perfect guys did exist. She knew one. And she'd stop at nothing to get him.

CHAPTER SEVENTEEN

It had been late after he dropped off Tiffin, so Mike hadn't gone to Mario's. When he got home, he went straight to his room, exhausted more from anger and frustration than from the game. He moaned with fatigue as he stretched out across his bed, but instead of falling asleep, he made a phone call. It was late, but maybe Darcy would still be up. He wanted to wish her a happy birthday. And he needed to talk.

"Hi, Mike!"

He smiled. "How'd you know it was me?"

"Well, if you'd enter the twenty-first century, you'd know cell phones have Caller ID." She had been on his case for weeks to get a cell phone.

"Can't argue with you there. Sorry I'm calling so late."

"Not a problem. I just came in from Mario's. Everyone was there to celebrate the win. Great game, by the way!"

"Thanks," he said, but he didn't want to talk about basketball. "I understand they were there to celebrate something else. Happy birthday."

"Thanks. I'm sorry you couldn't be there. I, uh, we missed you."

"I'm sorry, too. I planned on coming after Cliff told me it was your birthday, but something came up at the last minute."

Her voice took on concern. "You sound kind of down. I thought you'd still be wired from the game. Anything wrong?"

"Just tired, I guess."

"Well, that's understandable."

"Tell me all that happened at Mario's tonight." He knew Darcy would find this request strange, but he had to ask.

"Oh, you know. Nothing that special. Everyone was excited about the game. They're already making a lot of noise about winning the state title."

"Tell me more. Not about the game. About what you all did at Mario's. About what you got for your birthday."

Darcy was silent for a moment. "Are you sure? It's pretty boring —crazy kids doing mindless stuff."

"That's exactly what I want to hear. Don't leave out a thing." He began to unwind for the first time that day.

Darcy began slowly, but once she got started, she rattled on and on about the evening. The way the Sevens had decorated a corner of Mario's for her birthday, the cake that looked like a tennis court and its hideous green icing, the food fight between Cliff and Chris, the talk about the upcoming Harvest Moon Dance. The Sevens had pooled their money and bought her a gift card for some iTunes and one for coffee at MugShots.

Mike loved the way she giggled as she talked and how she seemed to enjoy reliving the events. He felt his eyelids growing heavy. "Thank you so much."

"For what?"

"For everything. See you tomorrow?"

"See you tomorrow," she said, sounding confused.

He rolled onto his side and fell asleep almost immediately. It was comforting to know that at least somewhere in this universe there were crazy teenagers doing mindless teenage stuff.

* * * *

Darcy and Megan sat in Darcy's car at The Tasty Treat in early November and sipped on their diet cherry vanilla Cokes. "You're not saying much tonight," Megan said matter-of-factly. "Something wrong between you and Mike?"

Darcy looked over at her friend and frowned. "Why would you say that?"

Megan fished a cherry out of her drink and popped it into her mouth. "Because if I hadn't known you for so long, I'd swear you're manic-depressive. One day you're bouncing off the walls with happiness, the next you're in the pits. But since I know you're not suffering from some sort of chemical imbalance, I can only assume the source of these mood swings is Mike."

Sometimes Megan could be so exasperating. Especially when she

70

was right. The past two weeks, Darcy had been riding an emotional roller coaster. One minute she was in a state of fairy tale bliss, the next she was experiencing zit-producing anxiety. She hadn't wanted to flip out over a guy, but it had happened. Regardless of what else occurred—a bad grade, a poor tennis score, problems with Tiffin—if Mike paid attention to her she was happy. If he was occupied with other things or didn't call, she was depressed.

"I'm sorry," she said. "I know I've been a royal pain. But this whole relationship with Mike is so frustrating."

"Why? You two seem to be hitting it off. Anyone can tell he likes you."

"Yeah, I think he does. I mean, we talk a lot in homeroom, and we meet whenever we can for lunch. He phones almost every night, but..."

"But what?"

"But I want more." Darcy crunched on some ice. "Do you realize Mike and I haven't been on a single date?   Since that afternoon at MugShots, we haven't even grabbed a snack together after school."

"When would you do it? Mike has basketball practice and you have tennis every afternoon. And now he has games every Tuesday and Friday night." Megan chewed on her straw, deep in thought. Her eyes lit up when she hit on a solution. "I know! Why don't you go out after a Friday night home game?"

"Mainly because he hasn't asked. Says he's too tired to be very good company."

Megan lifted her eyebrows. "Saturday nights?"

Darcy shrugged. "Same problem: hasn't asked." She stared straight ahead in thought. "I understand he's busy. On Saturdays he helps Aunt Rosie with chores, and on Sundays he takes her to church. Sunday afternoons he catches up on homework. But you'd think if he was really interested, he'd find time to ask me out."

Megan thought some more. "Well, his truck still isn't fixed. It's kind of hard to date on a bicycle."

"Whose side are you on?" Darcy asked. "He doesn't need you to make excuses for him. I've made it perfectly clear on several occasions Bee and I are available any time he needs a lift."

"Yeah, but it might be a little embarrassing for a guy to ask a girl out and then say, 'Could you drive?' You know, guys do have their pride." Megan wasn't cutting her any slack. "Anyway, if you want to go out on a Saturday night, ask him."

Darcy slapped herself on the forehead. "Duh…Why didn't I think of that? It must be nice to live in a world where everything is so simple."

Megan slurped the remainder of her drink. "Well, I'm not the one without a date on Saturday nights."

Talking to Megan was useless. Darcy refused to be any more forward than she had been. As far as she was concerned, she had done more than her share of the asking. If Mike couldn't take the hints, well, maybe he wasn't quite as quick in the romance department as he was on the basketball court. Or maybe she'd hit on the truth: maybe he wasn't that interested. She couldn't shake this last nagging thought—the true source of her bad moods.

Darcy dropped off Megan and drove home, trying not to obsess over her problem. At least Mike wasn't dating anyone else, despite the fact every girl in school would give up her phone for a week to go out with him. Okay, make that a day, but the point remained that Mike was every girl's dream. Besides having the face and body of a Hollywood hunk, Mike was genuinely kind. He always seemed to know exactly what girls wanted to hear, and he didn't try too hard to be cool.

In addition, he was the star athlete at Easton High. His near-supernatural ability on the basketball court was already attracting the attention of college scouts and—rumor had it—some professional ones. He had been dubbed the Winged Wonder because he moved up and down the court with the speed of the wind and he defied gravity when he went for lay-ups or dunks.

Mike had his male admirers, too, although they'd eat four-day-old road kill before they'd admit it. Chad, Cliff, and Chris discussed basketball non-stop at lunch, and what Mike had done in the previous game dominated their conversation. In between classes, the boys talked about outstanding plays Mike had made or how many three-pointers he hit. On *Sports Junkie*, a local radio program, there was much discussion regarding the way Mike was re-writing high school record books and a lot of speculation about the college offers he would receive.

Showered with such attention, any other guy would have trouble fitting his head through the neck of his jersey. But Mike remained down to earth. His celebrity status hadn't affected his attitude one bit. Of course, this added to his appeal.

Darcy lectured herself as she drove. She couldn't let down on her studies. Raising her ACT score a point or two could make a big difference in scholarship money. And two juniors were nipping at her heels, threatening to take her number one position on the tennis team, so she couldn't ease up on practice. With all this going on, she had to keep a level head. She shouldn't be thinking about Mike. But she did. Constantly.

CHAPTER EIGHTEEN

Mike half anticipated, half dreaded the day before him. Tonight was the Harvest Moon Dance, and evidently this was a big event at Easton High. Students—more specifically, girls—had been talking about it for weeks. Who they were going with, what they were wearing, how they would fix their hair, blah, blah, blah.

He was looking forward to spending a Saturday night with Darcy, but he'd like to skip the dance. This reluctance stemmed from the fact he'd never been to a school dance before and, quite honestly, didn't feel he'd missed anything. But he was keeping this information to himself. Some students already thought he was a freak of nature. If they knew he'd never been to a dance, they'd be certain he was.

"Mike," Aunt Rosie called from downstairs. "I'm leaving for my beauty appointment. I'll be back in an hour or so."

"Okay." Mike watched from his upstairs window as Aunt Rosie backed her old car out of the drive, barely missing the mailbox. Then he raced downstairs and turned on her dinosaur television set. He adjusted the knobs until the channel came in with a fuzzy, slightly distorted picture. The irony of watching MTV on the antiquated set didn't escape him. He never watched this station, but Megan—a veritable encyclopedia on the hottest rock stars, the latest hits, and the newest dances—talked about it constantly. So in a desperate attempt to learn some moves, he tuned in.

He watched the jerking, twisting dancers in the videos with horror. Is this what he was expected to do? He studied and analyzed the convoluted movements and tried to mimic them. After an hour, he was drenched with sweat and still looked as awkward as a Great Dane pup. Panic seized him. On the basketball court, he executed jumps and turns

75

which challenged the laws of physics, but no way would he ever learn motions like those in the videos—especially by tonight.

"Okay, okay, calm down," he told himself as he collapsed on the couch. If worse came to worst, he could always say he pulled a muscle at basketball practice and would have to sit out all the dances.

Aunt Rosie walked into the living room, and he jumped up and dove for the *Off* button on the TV. But he didn't reach it before she saw what was on the screen.

"Oh, honey," she said, "I'm sorry. I didn't mean to startle you."

"That's okay. I didn't hear you come in." He tried to act casual. "Your hair looks nice."

"Thank you, sweetie." She patted her silver curls. "What was that you were watching?"

He'd hoped to avoid this, but he might as well explain the whole story. Aunt Rosie listened sympathetically while he told of his predicament. When he finished, she reached up and pinched his cheek.

"Oh, honey, if that's all that's bothering you, why didn't you say something before? I can help you."

Doubtful, he watched her walk over to an ancient phonograph and put on an old 45 record. Fats Domino began belting out "My Blue Heaven." She extended her arms and beckoned him toward her. "I do a pretty mean jitterbug if I do say so myself," she said with a wink.

That evening, Mike peered out the living room window. The minute he saw Darcy drive up, he hurried to her car and opened the door. He couldn't help staring. She had worn her hair soft and flowing around her face, and her blouse, the color and sheen of a sapphire, intensified the blue in her hazel eyes. He had never understood why pretty girls wore heavy make-up, and he liked the fact Darcy never did. Something she had done tonight, though, gave her face a special glow. And she smelled like autumn.

He stood beside the car as if he'd taken root and thought surely Darcy must know how beautiful she is. She had probably been told hundreds of times, and she attracted admiring glances wherever she went. What mattered most, though, was that she know how beautiful she was inside. But no one—not he, not friends, not anyone—could tell her. She would have to discover that for herself.

"Mike, are you okay?"

The words yanked him back to the moment. "I'm fine," he said and cleared his throat. "And you look fantastic." He put his arm around her shoulder. "Come in the house and meet Aunt Rosie."

He ushered Darcy into the living room of the farmhouse and offered her a seat on the worn, overstuffed sofa. He called to Aunt Rosie, anxious for the two of them to meet. Aunt Rosie had a way of making everyone feel at home.

Aunt Rosie bustled into the living room, smiling and drying her hands on her apron. Flour smudged one of her cheeks. "Honey, it's so good to finally meet you."

"It's great to meet you, too." Darcy began to rise, but Aunt Rosie motioned for her to sit.

"No, no don't get up. We don't stand on formalities around here." She sat on the couch beside Darcy. "I couldn't wait to meet you. Mike talks about you constantly."

"He does?"

"Oh my, yes. And he says the nicest things." She squinted behind her wire-rimmed glasses and studied Darcy's face. "Mike, you're right. This young lady is—what did you say?—'absolutely stunning.'"

Both Darcy and Aunt Rosie looked at Mike. He tugged at his shirt collar and shuffled his feet. A buzzer going off in the kitchen saved him.

"Oh, goodness, that's my pie!" Aunt Rosie sprang from the couch and ran to the kitchen.

Darcy looked at Mike with a raised eyebrow. "Absolutely stunning, huh?"

Mike laughed nervously.

Aunt Rosie returned to the living room. "Could I get you two to sample my apple pie? See if it's any good?"

The divine aroma would have tempted an anorexic supermodel, but Mike and Darcy declined, explaining they were already late.

Aunt Rosie walked over to Darcy and gave her a hug. "As far as I'm concerned, if I've met you once, you're family. So you come back any time you want. Don't wait for an invitation."

Darcy said good-by and assured her she would come back soon and often.

In the car on the way to the dance, Mike looked over at Darcy as she drove. A puzzled expression covered her face. "Something wrong?"

he asked.

"No. Not really. I just can't get over the feeling I've met Aunt Rosie somewhere before."

When they arrived at the school, Darcy and Mike met Megan, Chad and the rest of the Sevens at the door of the cafeteria, and everyone went in together.

"Impressive," Mike said as he looked around. "Are you sure this is the dungeon?"

Darcy smiled with evident satisfaction and explained she and her decorating committee had worked all day. Their efforts had transformed the drab cafeteria into an authentic country barn. She pointed out the stalls, pumpkins, hay bales, corn stalks, and the live cow.

Always one for details, Chad spoke. "Uh, what happens if the cow decides to... uh...relieve itself?"

"Not my problem," Darcy said. "I'm not on the clean-up committee."

In sharp contrast to the country setting, rock music blasted from giant speakers. Mike peered out at the dance floor. Relief flooded him when he noticed most of the dancers simply stood in one place, shuffling their feet and twisting their torsos. He could do that.

Then the deejay played a slow song. The harsh fluorescent bulbs dimmed, and above the dance floor, twinkle lights gave the effect of a star-studded sky.

Mike spotted Tiffin and Reese. They were dancing in a dark corner, apart from the other students. There was not room for air between their bodies. Reese had both hands on Tiffin's backside and pressed her tightly against him as they writhed to the music. Mike detected indifference on Tiffin's face. Reese's face projected his customary scowl.

Mike observed the other couples swaying together on the dance floor. He determined he could do that as well. In fact, it looked kind of nice. He took Darcy's hand and led her to the middle of the crowd. Then he placed both his hands around her waist. She moved in close to him and leaned her head against his chest. Their bodies moved to the gentle rhythm of the music. Mike closed his eyes and imagined himself in heaven.

* * * *

The minute Mike's arms encircled her waist, Darcy hoped he

would never take them away. Nothing had ever felt so right. She wanted to stay in this place, exactly like this, for the rest of her life. Mike seemed to know by instinct where and how to hold her. He didn't grope or place his hands in embarrassing places. But he wasn't awkward and stiff, either, which would make them both feel uncomfortable and self-conscious.

Also, it didn't hurt that Mike was a good dancer. Of course, this came as no surprise to Darcy. She had seen his grace and agility on the basketball court. It was easy to follow his lead as he moved to the music. In his embrace, Darcy closed her eyes and relaxed, surrendering to the mood created by the soft music and fairy lights.

Darcy wished the deejay would play slow songs all night, but she also enjoyed the fast ones. Mike's sense of rhythm kept him from looking geeky or like he was trying too hard. Fast music or slow, Darcy mostly liked the fact she and Mike danced every dance together.

After the last song, they left the cafeteria hand in hand. Darcy couldn't remember a more perfect night, and she hoped it wasn't at an end. They had been surrounded by people the entire time. Now she wanted them to be alone.

"That was fun," Mike said as they strolled toward Darcy's car.

"You say that like you're surprised. What were you expecting?"

"Well, to tell the truth, I was a little worried. I haven't gone to a lot of parties. I was afraid my dance moves would be kind of rusty."

"Let me assure you, your dancing skills are excellent." Darcy gave Mike a sideways glance. "But I'm not buying that 'not a party guy' line."

Mike put his arm around Darcy's shoulder and gave her a good-natured hug. Then he pulled her closer to him.

Darcy's knees quivered and her insides turned to mush. She had to think of some way for this night to continue. This was a new predicament for her. Usually, she was the one trying to think of ways to turn down invitations like the one she was about to suggest. "You want to go by The Tasty Treat and get a Coke?" she asked. It was a pitiful plan, but it would allow her and Mike to talk privately for a while longer. If she was lucky, maybe Mike would come up with something more romantic.

CHAPTER NINETEEN

Another couple left the dance the same time as Mike and Darcy. Tiffin and Reese walked across the parking lot, Reese gripping the back of her neck with one hand.

"Hey, baby, you thirsty?" Reese nuzzled her shoulder.

Tiffin pulled away from him. "Yeah, it was kind of hot in there."

"Well, I've got some beer iced down in the back of my truck. Why don't we head out to the lake and—"

A battered black muscle car rumbled up beside them and stopped. Deep bass sounds reverberated from inside it. The driver rolled down the black-tinted window. "Hey, Reese, need some 'groceries'?"

Reese rubbed his chin. "Yeah, I could use some."

"Well, I happen to know where they're havin' a sale tonight. Get in."

Reese turned to Tiffin. "I'll call you' later," he said without the slightest hint of apology.

Tiffin shrugged. "Whatever."

Reese climbed into the passenger seat, and the car sped away.

This scenario wasn't anything new to Tiffin, and she was more relieved than annoyed. Maybe she could hook up with some of her friends and have fun for a change.

She walked in the direction of her car. On dates with Reese, Tiffin often drove herself and met up with him. It worked better for situations like tonight, and those occurred frequently.

Almost to her car, Tiffin pulled her cell phone from her purse and punched some numbers. "Hey, Angie. Where's the party?"

Angie was giving directions to the field party location, when Tiffin looked across the parking lot and saw Mike and Darcy. Mike rested his arm across Darcy's shoulder, and her head lay against him. Their laughter floated on the air as they walked toward Darcy's car.

Tiffin's pulse raced and her eyes narrowed. "Okay, never mind," she said, interrupting Angie. "Change of plans. Talk to you later." She hung up and chunked her phone into her purse. "Well, isn't that sweet?" she muttered to herself.

Tiffin had watched the couple all night and had seen the way Mike held Darcy when they danced—as if she was a fragile butterfly or a porcelain figurine. Then Tiffin recalled the way Reese had groped her. Such a contrast to the way she heard Mike and Darcy talking and laughing, so at ease with each other. Every girl in the room had wanted to dance with Mike, but he'd focused all his attention on Darcy.

Tiffin had disliked Darcy since the first day she met her. It wasn't that Darcy was mean or stuck up. She was just so annoying. How could someone in sixth grade be such a dweeb? Unlike Tiffin and most of her friends, Darcy lived with both parents who obviously needed to get a life. They meddled in everything Darcy did. They wouldn't even allow her to attend boy/girl parties unless they knew the chaperones and trusted them. Then there was the way Darcy had dressed. You would've thought she was at a Catholic girls' school. She didn't wear a uniform or anything like that, but her outfits didn't reveal the least bit of anything boys would find interesting.

Right from the start, Tiffin had made it clear Darcy wasn't nearly cool enough to fit in with her crowd. Then—just because she could— Tiffin had worked to make sure Darcy wouldn't fit in anywhere.

Tiffin might have succeeded if it hadn't been for that busybody Megan. For some reason, Megan had appointed herself Darcy's personal watchdog, and she guarded her fiercely. Where Darcy would back down and say, "Let it go, it's no big deal," Megan would jump in ready to fight anyone who attacked her friend. But by the time middle school ended, Darcy didn't need Megan defending her. Nothing Tiffin did or said intimidated Darcy anymore. Most of the time, Darcy ignored her. And Darcy had plenty of friends—in fact, a lot more than Tiffin. Tiffin couldn't believe so many people fell for Darcy's innocent little daddy's-girl act. And now, Mike had fallen for it, too.

Jealousy, pain, and desperation whirled in Tiffin's brain like ingredients in a blender. She clenched her fists until her nails dug into her palms. What did Mike see in Darcy? She was a jock and a bookworm

—about as sexy as a nun. And although she wasn't chubby anymore, she still wasn't very pretty—at least not with her boring make-up and clothes.

A tight knot formed in Tiffin's stomach. Seeing Mike's arm draped around Darcy's shoulders reminded Tiffin of how little she mattered to anyone. These days, monthly child support checks were the only indication her father knew she existed. Those same checks informed her she was no more than a meal ticket for Dodie. And Reese—well, it didn't take a genius to figure out she was only a piece of property to him. Until Mike had rescued her that first time, it seemed like forever since someone had really cared about her.

Her breath came in shallow, rapid pulses. At seventeen, she faced a frightening future. A future with all the promise of a jail sentence, a future she was desperate to avoid. Mike offered the only hope of a pardon, and no way was she standing by and letting Saint Darcy ruin it.

Tiffin thought about how she had disliked Darcy since the first day she met her. It wasn't that Darcy was mean or stuck up. She was just so annoying. How could someone in sixth grade be such a dweeb? Unlike Tiffin and most of her friends, Darcy lived with both parents who obviously needed to get a life. They meddled in everything Darcy did. They wouldn't even allow her to attend boy/girl parties unless they knew the chaperones and trusted them. Then there was the way Darcy dressed. You would've thought she was at a Catholic girls' school. She didn't wear a uniform or anything like that, but her outfits didn't reveal the least bit of anything boys would find interesting.

Right from the start, Tiffin had made it clear Darcy wasn't nearly cool enough to fit in with her crowd. Then—just because she could— Tiffin had worked to make sure Darcy wouldn't fit in anywhere.

Tiffin might have succeeded if it hadn't been for that busybody Megan. For some reason, Megan appointed herself Darcy's personal watchdog, and she guarded her fiercely. Where Darcy would back down and say, "Let it go, it's no big deal," Megan would jump in ready to fight anyone who attacked her friend. But by the time middle school ended, Darcy didn't need Megan defending her. Nothing Tiffin did or said intimidated Darcy anymore. Most of the time, Darcy ignored her. And Darcy had plenty of friends—in fact, a lot more than Tiffin. Tiffin couldn't believe so many people fell for Darcy's innocent little daddy's-girl act. And now, Mike had fallen for it, too.

Tonight, seeing Darcy with Mike reminded her of all that was wrong in her life. Mike was her one hope of ever gaining love or security . And she knew Mike cared for her. Why else would he always be coming to her rescue? No way was she standing by and letting Saint Darcy destroy her only chance of happiness.

Tiffin's hair flew in every direction as she leaned over and shook her head. She ripped the neck of her sheer blouse, causing it to hang off one shoulder and expose her red bra strap. Then she smudged her eye make-up to look as if she'd been crying and ran in the direction of Mike and Darcy. When she reached them, she grabbed Mike's hand in both of hers and tugged on it. With cunning she had perfected through years of practice, she whimpered, "Mike, I need your help."

For a moment, she thought Mike wasn't going to fall for her performance. He pulled his hand free and stared at her face. Then his eyes fell to her torn shirt. His chest sunk as he released a sigh and turned to Darcy with a helpless look. "I'll make this up to you...I promise. But I have to go."

As they walked away from Darcy, Tiffin was grateful for the darkness that hid her satisfied smile. She wasn't the only one who'd been stranded in the parking lot tonight.

* * * *

Darcy stood in the parking lot, too dazed and confused to move. How could, in the blink of an eye, her dream night turn into such a nightmare? Not two minutes before she was trying to think of perfect ways to end this night. This had not been one of options.

At her car, Darcy's hands shook as she fumbled in her purse for You don't understand at allher keys. With another car, she would have been kicking the door or pounding on the roof. But this was Bee. She would no more treat Bee like that than she would Megan. There had to be a better way to defuse the powder keg that was about to explode inside her.

On the drive home, Darcy was too angry to cry. At this moment she and Mike should be parked somewhere, snuggled close together, counting the stars. Instead, she was alone, driving herself home, and Tiffin was somewhere putting the moves on Mike.

To calm herself, Darcy thought of the game she and Mike had often played since that evening at MugShots. "If you could go anywhere in the world right now, where would you go?" he would ask, whenever he sensed she was worried or stressed. Sometimes she named far-off, little-known places like Umbria. Sometimes the places were common and comfortable like The Tasty Treat for an ice cream, and sometimes she'd ramble off a list of places. But her final answer was always "beyond the farthest star."

Tonight not even that destination appealed to her. There was only one place she wanted to go: Tiffin's house. She'd go there and...and... put a depilatory in Tiffin's shampoo bottle.

Hmm. That helped a little. What else would she do?

She'd contaminate Tiffin's shoes with that nasty toenail fungus.

No, wait! She'd put poison ivy in all of Tiffin's push-up bras.

The remainder of the way home, Darcy brainstormed ways to get even with Tiffin. By the time she pulled into her driveway, she was feeling a lot better.

* * * *

Mike had once again offered to drive Tiffin's car. "I was surprised to see you and Reese at the dance," he said on the way to her house. "I thought the Hawks usually threw their own party when the school sponsored one."

"Yeah, they do, but since this is kind of a special dance, the Hawks are giving an 'after-party' party. They're all meeting somewhere right now."

"If you and Reese were on a date, why do you have your car at school?"

Tiffin smoothed her hair and touched up her make-up in the visor mirror. She explained why the two of them always met somewhere on their dates and what had happened right after they left the dance tonight. "So for the millionth time," she complained, "the jerk left me standing in the parking lot, stranded like—"

Tiffin froze in mid-sentence. Her expression told Mike she realized what she'd just confessed.

He raised an eyebrow. "So if Reese left with his friend right after the dance, when did he rough you up?"

Tiffin tried to turn her blunder into a joke. "Busted," she said with a guilty grin. Then she reached over and massaged the back of Mike's neck. "Please don't be mad. I had to think of a way for you and me to be together. At school Reese and Darcy are always around. There's no time for us to talk. Why don't we—"

Mike reached up and snatched Tiffin's hand from his neck. "Don't! I..." He stopped and rubbed his forehead. "Look, Tiffin, I'm glad to help you when you're in trouble. In fact, I want to help you. But you're a big girl. I'm sure you've heard the story of the boy who cried 'wolf.' It's a dangerous thing to do."

"Okay, okay," Tiffin grumbled. She pouted for a few minutes, then tried another approach. She hung her head and spoke with a whine. "I'm sorry, Mike. Don't be mad. Let's go somewhere, and I'll buy you a Coke. I want us to be friends."

Mike wasn't falling for another of her tricks. "I don't think so." He stared at the road and gave the engine more gas. "I'm tired. I'm going to my house. You can drive yourself home from there."

They rode the rest of the way without exchanging a word. In his driveway, Mike got out of Tiffin's car and slammed the door. He charged up the steps of the farmhouse and went inside without so much as a backward glance.

* * * *

Tiffin scooted into the driver's seat. This was Saturday. As far as she was concerned, the night was young. She backed out of the drive and steered her car in the direction of the field party.

CHAPTER TWENTY

When the alarm buzzed, Darcy rolled over and covered her head with the pillow. She'd never had a hangover, but it couldn't be any worse than what she was experiencing right now. She hadn't slept for two nights, her head was pounding, and any minute she was going to hurl.

The Sunday morning before, she'd resolved not to speak to Mike when he called that day. She'd had no trouble keeping that resolution. Mike hadn't called. Why was *he* giving *her* the silent treatment? She was the one who'd been deserted.

Well, two could play at this game.

Darcy took extra care getting ready for school. What was that famous line—looking good is the best revenge? She wore a turquoise knit top under a black suede jacket and tucked her skinny jeans into black leather boots. Applying her make-up took extra time. The dark circles beneath her eyes refused to go away.

In homeroom, Darcy told Megan of her plan to flirt with other boys and ignore Mike all day.

"Hmmm. Good luck with that," Megan said.

Darcy watched the door. When Reese came in alone, Darcy turned to Megan. "What's that all about?"

"I heard Tiffin telling some of her friends she and her mom were going to Las Vegas for Thanksgiving. Guess they got an early start."

The next person to come through the door was Matt Spencer. Darcy called to him, "Hey, Matt, come sit over here." She pointed to the desk behind her. Matt had had a crush on Darcy since seventh grade. He was smart and nice looking, but he was shy.

Matt settled into the desk, and Darcy gave him her most

charming smile. "Hi, Matt. Were you at the dance on Saturday?"

Matt's face reddened, and he averted his eyes from Darcy's face. "I was there for a little while," he mumbled. "The music was too loud, so I left."

"That's too bad. I looked for you so we could dance. I guess you'd already gone." Darcy patted his arm. "Save me a dance next time, okay?"

Matt gave her a tight-lipped grin, but said nothing.

Darcy's plan to flirt in front of Mike and ignore him fell through because he never showed up at school. He was absent all day Monday and still gone on Tuesday, a game day and the last day before Thanksgiving break. Darcy's anger turned to concern then alarm. Mike wouldn't miss a game unless something was seriously wrong.

On Thanksgiving morning Darcy's mother rolled out pie dough while Darcy chopped celery and onions for dressing. "You haven't said much the past couple of days," her mother said. "Something bothering you?"

Darcy hadn't mentioned the incident at the dance to her parents. She knew they would immediately side with her, and she didn't want them mad at Mike. Not yet, anyway. And she hated to bring up the subject of Tiffin. Tiffin had caused enough turmoil in the Dunn household back in middle school days.

But Darcy welcomed the chance to talk to her mother about Mike's disappearance. Carol was a counselor at a local health facility. Maybe she could offer an explanation for Mike's strange behavior.

"No one at school has seen or heard from him? Not his coach or his teammates?" Carol asked.

Darcy shook her head.

"Hmmm." Lines of concern creased Carol's brow. "And you say Aunt Rosie's not home, either?"

"Nope. I tried calling her Tuesday night and no one answered. Then yesterday I drove out to her house. Everything was locked up tight."

"Well, I wouldn't worry too much at this point. Everything gets hectic this time of year. Maybe they were so busy making travel plans, Mike forgot to mention them to you." Carol wiped her hands on a paper towel. "If anything bad had happened—like an accident or something— you would've heard by now."

Darcy chopped furiously. If she started to cry, she could blame the tears on the onions.

Darcy and her mom worked all day in the kitchen, preparing a huge meal for family and guests. But when everyone sat down at the table, Darcy couldn't eat a bite. She pushed her food around on her plate and hoped no one would notice.

With the meal finished and company gone, Darcy moped around her house. She tried not to think about Mike, but there was nothing else to occupy her time. Megan had gone skiing with her family, and the rest of the Sevens were out of town visiting relatives. Darcy attempted a little homework, but found it impossible to concentrate. She finally resorted to chick flicks but gave up on those, too. In the movies, the boy and girl always got together despite all the obstacles. Darcy wasn't sure she was destined for such a happy ending.

For the first time she could remember, Darcy wanted the holidays to end. On Sunday evening, she had hit rock bottom and was digging when her phone rang. Certain it was Megan, Darcy didn't check the caller's name. "Hello," she grumbled.

"Darcy?"

CHAPTER TWENTY-ONE

"Mike!" Tears stung Darcy's eyes and she could hardly keep her voice from shaking. "How are you? Where have you been?" *So much for the silent treatment.*

"I'm sorry I haven't called you." Mike sounded tired. "Early Sunday morning my dad got in touch and needed me immediately, so I didn't have time to tell you before I left. I would've called you from home, but...it's in a pretty remote area."

Must be very remote not to have phone service, Darcy thought. But she wouldn't worry about that now. Mike's return erased the torment his absence had caused.

"Is everything okay at home?" Darcy asked.

"Yeah, things are fine. I can't remember if I've told you this before, but it's difficult for my dad and me to get together. We can't see each other often, so when he calls, I drop everything and go."

"Well, I'm glad nothing was wrong. I worried about you. Leaving so suddenly without any word."

There was a short silence. "Listen, Darcy," Mike said, "I hate the way I ran off after the dance. I was going to call you Sunday morning and explain, but, like I said, I didn't get the chance. It's not something I want to talk about over the phone, and I don't think we'll have enough time at lunch. I know it's a school night, but can we meet somewhere tomorrow evening after basketball practice? I'll buy you dinner."

"How can I refuse an offer like that?" Darcy tried to control her excitement.

"Good. We'll make plans tomorrow in homeroom." Mike added softly, "One more thing. I've missed you. I can't wait to see you tomorrow."

"I've missed you, too."

Darcy had experienced one of the worst weeks of her life, but the suffering was worth it. At last Mike had asked her out.

The following evening, Darcy and Mike met at Ted's Diner, where the stainless steel and Formica decor provided the perfect atmosphere for the tasteless food. But Ted's prices were reasonable, and the orange, vinyl-upholstered booths offered plenty of privacy for talking.

Darcy was sitting in a corner booth studying the menu when Mike joined her. Out of breath, he slipped into the seat across from her. His hair was still wet from the shower, and he smelled faintly of BENGAY.

"Tough practice?" Darcy asked.

Mike twisted his neck from side to side and rotated his shoulders. "Coach decided we needed to run off all that Thanksgiving turkey and dressing. We did fifty push-ups and ran thirty suicides before we started drills. I don't know why they're called suicides. Should be *homicides*. I think the coach is trying to kill us."

They ate their hamburgers and fries, and Darcy filled Mike in on the previous holidays' activities. Not wanting to sound like a total loser, she made them out to be more enjoyable than they were. She and Mike talked about school, basketball, tennis, and the approaching Christmas holidays.

Darcy's spirits plunged at the thought of winter break. Would Mike go back home for Christmas vacation? If a week's separation sent her into the throes of despair, what would two weeks do? But she dismissed this line of thought. No point in borrowing misery. Right now, she would enjoy the moment.

The waitress cleared the table of everything but their drinks. When she walked away, Mike took Darcy's hand in both of his. "You have no idea how much I've missed you," he said.

Darcy chewed the inside of her cheek. Oh, yeah. She had an idea.

"And I owe you an apology," he continued.

No argument there. Darcy said nothing.

Then Mike lifted her hand to his lips and lightly kissed her palm.

Darcy suppressed a slight shiver. She wondered how such an innocent gesture could melt her icy resolve to let him squirm his way through an explanation.

"First, I'm sorry for the way I ran off and left you in the parking lot," Mike said. "I had a great time at the dance, and I was looking forward to spending more time with you that night."

"I was looking forward to that, too."

"When Tiffin ran up to us, I didn't have time to think. I reacted the way I did because of some incidents in the past."

"Like what?"

Mike sat silently as if carefully choosing his words. "I don't have to tell you Tiffin doesn't always make the best decisions," he said finally.

"That's a given."

Mike smiled at her response but then grew serious. "On a couple of occasions, I happened to be in places where I could help her. They were tight predicaments where she could have been hurt." He grimaced and let out a sigh. "I don't know. Now she's come to rely on me. Probably more than she should. But I can't walk away and not at least try to do something.

"I know Tiffin has been horrible to you in the past, and I don't blame you for the way you feel about her." He pressed his lips together as he thought. "I'm not asking you to be her best friend, but please understand I have to help her if I can."

Darcy knew she should listen to Mike's explanation with an open mind and an open heart. Since the locker incident, Tiffin hadn't harassed Darcy and, in fact, appeared to be avoiding her. But whatever progress Darcy had made toward letting go of the past took a giant step backward the night of the dance. And there were still those threats Darcy had overheard on the first day of school.

"Mike, you're a good person, and I understand you don't want to see Tiffin hurt. Believe it or not, I don't want her hurt, either." Ice cubes clinked against glass as Darcy stirred her drink with the straw. "But sometimes, you seem kind of naïve. I don't think you realize how scheming and manipulative Tiffin can be, and she's capable of causing a lot of harm. She's come to rely on you because you've let her. You don't have to be her guardian angel, you know."

A hint of panic flashed across Mike's face. Then his eyes bore into Darcy's with almost painful intensity. "If I don't help her, who will?"

The question made no sense to Darcy. She had no idea what kind of trouble Tiffin was in, but surely someone other than Mike could come to her aid. She had friends and family, didn't she? And what about

Reese? No one messed with Tiffin if Reese was around.

Organizing her jumbled thoughts into some kind of response would take time. Mike could think she was mean and petty, but Darcy wasn't going to make a promise she couldn't keep. And right now she couldn't promise to accept Mike's caretaker role.

"I need time to think," Darcy said. She clenched her teeth to keep her chin from quivering. Trying to make a fast getaway so Mike wouldn't see her cry, she gathered up her purse and slid across the booth.

Mike caught her arm before she stood. "I understand," he said.

But Darcy knew he didn't. He couldn't. No way could Mike understand it was Darcy, not Tiffin, who needed guarding.

She drove home with Bee's top down. Maybe the frosty evening air would settle the whirlwind in her head. Mike hadn't revealed any details about Tiffin's trouble, and Darcy respected him for that. Most guys gossiped as much as girls. Maybe more. That was just one of the ways Mike was different.

Darcy didn't kid herself. She had first been attracted to Mike because of his looks. The reason she grew to care for him, though, was his goodness—his humility, his selfless spirit, his kindness to others. Asking him not to help Tiffin was like asking a bird not to fly or a fish not to swim. Helping others was what Mike did. If she loved Mike, she would have to accept that.

This last thought caught Darcy by surprise. The word *love* had come out of nowhere. She was only eighteen, still in high school. Much too young to be thinking about love. But in spite of her common sense arguments, Darcy admitted the truth. She loved Mike Albright.

CHAPTER TWENTY-TWO

Mike picked up his phone on the first ring. After he said hello, he heard someone draw a deep breath.

"Okay, I can't make any guarantees, but I'll try my best," Darcy said. Then she shifted into a monotone voice, like a kid making a forced apology. "I'll try to be supportive of you and more accepting of Tiffin. But don't expect us to be buying Best Friends Forever necklaces at the mall any time soon." She hung up without waiting for his reply.

Aunt Rosie walked into Mike's room to deliver clean laundry and found him sitting on the edge of his bed, staring at the phone in his hand.

"What's the matter, dear?" she asked. "Bad connection?"

"The connection is fine." Happiness flooded Mike's heart. "I heard exactly what I needed to."

* * * *

"Will you be going home for Christmas?" Darcy hoped Mike didn't detect her worry as they sat in a booth at MugShots and discussed the upcoming holidays. The coach had cancelled basketball practice this afternoon, giving them a rare opportunity to meet after school.

"No, I'll be staying here," Mike said to Darcy's great relief. "Christmas is the busiest time of year for my dad. If I joined him, we couldn't spend much time together. So it'll be Aunt Rosie and me for the holidays." He dropped his chin, stuck out his lower lip, and pouted. "Yes, Aunt Rosie and me," he said. "Just the two of us." He heaved a dramatic sigh. Keeping his chin down, he raised his eyes to meet Darcy's. "Unless some kind-hearted person agrees to spend Christmas afternoon with us."

Darcy's family and relatives ate their turkey dinner and attended church services on Christmas Eve. On Christmas morning they opened their gifts. By that afternoon, the company would be gone, her dad would be stretched out and snoring on the couch, and her mom would be watching *Miracle on 34th Street* for at least the thirty-fourth time. Her heart racing with joy, Darcy agreed to be that kindhearted person.

The first Saturday of winter break, Darcy strolled with Megan through the mall. The weeks before break—filled with tests, term papers, parties, and programs—had stressed Darcy to the max. Now she was ready to relax and enjoy the season. She looked around, absorbing the sights and sounds. Manic shoppers crowded the corridors and stores, gaudy lights and fake greenery hung from every fixture, and Bing Crosby crooned "I'm Dreaming of a White Christmas" from the public address system. At the Santa Land Depot, kids shrieked from either excitement or mortal fear while they waited in a long line to see Santa.

People could say what they wanted about Christmas being too commercial or losing its true meaning. Darcy didn't agree. She loved everything about it: the parties, the music, the food. And she, for one, didn't forget the reason for the season. The nativity scene her mother displayed on their sofa table every year was Darcy's favorite decoration. As a little girl, she would recite the Christmas story and move the figurines around like characters in a play. She especially loved the angel with its beautiful face, flowing white gown, and delicate wings. But growing older, Darcy had come to love its message also: "Fear not, I bring you glad tidings of great joy!" Who could possibly remain depressed or discouraged on hearing words so full of hope, delivered by such a heavenly creature?

Christmas was the one time of year Darcy enjoyed shopping. She liked getting gifts, and she enjoyed giving them. But when Megan asked her what she was giving Mike for Christmas, her enjoyment hit a dead end. "I have no earthly idea. I don't know why it's so difficult to shop for him. It's not like he's the guy who has everything."

"True," Megan said. "In fact, he's not like a guy who has *anything*. Right now he doesn't even have a car since his truck is still being fixed." The girls walked past GameStop, only glancing at the displays. "And he has no cell phone or computer, so that rules out a video game or iTunes."

Darcy groaned. "It drives me crazy that he doesn't own a phone. Says he doesn't need one. Can you believe it? He doesn't seem to want anything."

The girls stopped in front of the American Eagle window. Megan pointed to a mannequin dressed in a zipped hoodie and low-slung, ripped jeans which exposed plaid boxers underneath. "What about getting him some clothes? He always wears the same thing over and over."

Darcy eyed the outfit and tried to picture Mike wearing it. Somehow it didn't seem like a fit. "I know. Every day he wears his standard uniform: jeans, tee shirt, Nikes. On cold days, he *accessorizes* with his old army jacket."

"Well," Megan reasoned, "it's not like he needs clothes to look good." She slapped her hand over her mouth. "Wait! That came out totally wrong. What I meant was Mike would look hot in anything he wore—even my dad's sweater vest and orthopedic shoes."

Darcy laughed at Megan, whose face turned as red as Rudolph's nose. Darcy knew what Megan meant, but she still didn't know what to get Mike for Christmas.

With her body clock still on school time, Darcy rose early on the first Monday of Christmas break. She looked out the window to discover over a foot of powdery snow had fallen during the night. Easton usually had two or three light snowfalls a year, but seldom one like this. She was peering at the silent, transformed world when the revelation came to her. At last she knew what she would give Mike for Christmas.

"Hello." Mike's greeting was followed by a huge yawn.

"What are your plans for today?" Darcy asked.

"Who is this and do you know what time it is?"

This was the nearest to grumpy Mike had ever been, but Darcy didn't apologize. She didn't have time for small talk this morning. "You know very well who this is, and it's 6:30. Answer my question."

"Well, my plans *were* to replace some shingles on Aunt Rosie's roof, but those have been cancelled. You have anything in mind?"

"Sure do. Pick you up at 1:00. Dress warm."

"Where are we—"

"See you then," Darcy said and hung up.

She slipped on her favorite house shoes, the fuzzy, yellow Tweety Bird ones, and put her ski parka over her flannel pajamas.

When she switched on the attic light, Darcy could see her breath. "Br-r-r." She rubbed her mittened hands together and shivered as she surveyed the clutter. "Where is it? I know it's stored up here some—there it is!"

CHAPTER TWENTY-THREE

Darcy spied the Flexible Flyer in a corner behind some luggage. Careful not to put her foot through drywall, she hauled the sled across the attic floor and down the stairs. It was a little rusty and in need of some heavy-duty cleaning, but otherwise it was perfect.

Darcy spent the rest of the morning in the freezing garage, working like a crazed elf. She polished and oiled the old sled until it gleamed like a new one, but the hard part was wrapping it.

Darcy stood back to admire her handiwork and burst out laughing. The oblong pile of paper and ribbon looked like an explosion in a crafts store. Oh well, it would be coming off very soon.

At 12:45, the temperature hovered a little above freezing, but the sun shone brightly, and only a light snow was falling. The sand trucks had made driving possible, so Darcy loaded up the sled. She had some difficulty at first but finally figured out a way to fit it into Bee's backseat.

Darcy drove carefully to Aunt Rosie's house, never going over ten miles an hour. She reached up often to wipe snowflakes off her goggles. People were staring at her. What was their problem? Hadn't they seen a convertible with the top down before?

Mike was at her car by the time Darcy turned off the engine in Aunt Rosie's drive. "What's this?" He laughed and pointed to the strange object sticking out of Bee's back seat.

"This," Darcy said, "is your Christmas present. Show a little respect, please."

Together they lugged the gift into the house where a welcoming fire burned in the fireplace and mouth-watering smells drifted from the kitchen.

"Aunt Rosie's doing her Christmas baking," Mike explained as he helped Darcy remove her parka.

Darcy peeked into the dining room. Desserts of every kind covered the entire table. She looked out of the corner of her eye at Mike. "So Aunt Rosie's making all of this for the two of you, huh?"

Mike mumbled something about "maybe a couple of relatives" and changed the subject. "Do I have to wait till Christmas to open this?"

"No. As a matter of fact, you have to open it right now."

Mike tore into the wrapping. When he uncovered the sled, he sat back on his heels and let out a whoop.

"Do you like it?" Darcy held her breath.

"I love it!" Mike grabbed the sled and turned it every which way. He examined it like a little boy inspecting a new toy truck. "It's awesome! Let's go try it out right now."

"That was my plan."

With the sled once again protruding from the back seat, Darcy and Mike searched for a place to test it. Hammond Park was humming with activity, but Darcy drove right past.

"Aren't you going to stop here?" Mike asked.

"Not today." All of Darcy's friends would be at the park, using inner tubes, garbage can lids, old kiddy pools—anything they could find for makeshift sleds—to race down the gently sloping hills. Normally, she would be right in the middle of the fun, but she and Mike rarely had time together. Today it would be the two of them.

Darcy remembered a similar outing years ago in which she and her dad had discovered the best sledding hill in Easton. She drove to a church not far from her house and pulled into the deserted parking lot. After she and Mike wrestled the sled from the back seat, Darcy grabbed Mike's hand and led him behind the church. The two of them crunched through the snow and dragged the sled behind them. She had never disclosed this location to anyone, so today she and Mike had it all to themselves.

"Have you ever been sledding before?" Darcy asked.

"No, not much snow where I'm from."

"That's weird. I thought you said you were from up North."

Mike mentioned something about "unusual atmospheric conditions." Before Darcy could ask him anything else, he climbed onto the sled. "Maybe you could give me some pointers."

Darcy explained to Mike how to steer with his feet and body weight. He held the rope and positioned his feet, and Darcy gave him a shove which sent him hooting and hollering down the hill. Near the bottom he hit a bump. The sled went one direction and Mike went another, soaring spread eagle through the air.

Darcy hugged her stomach and fell over in the snow laughing. She knew she wouldn't hurt Mike's ego, although she suspected other parts of him would be in pain for quite a while.

Mike jumped up, brushed off the snow, and trudged back up the hill, pulling the sled. "I'm ready to go again," he said. "But this time, Miss Iditarod, you're going with me."

"Oh, no, Nanuk of the North." Darcy wagged her index finger in front of his face. "You need a few more—correction—a *lot* more practice runs before I join you."

"Chicken." Mike squawked and flapped his elbows. "I'm a fast learner. I'm ninety-nine percent sure I have the hang of it now."

"Yeah, it's that one percent that's bothering me," Darcy said, but she climbed onto the sled.

Mike smiled deviously and pulled her to the edge of the slope.

"I'm not sure I like that smile." Darcy gripped the sides of the sled.

"I'm not sure you should." With those words, Mike gave a giant push and jumped on behind her. He put his arms around her and grabbed the rope as they went zooming down the hill. Darcy screamed in excitement and terror.

Sitting on the sled in Mike's arms, Darcy was lightheaded with happiness. If anyone had asked her at that moment where in the world she wanted to go, her answer would've been immediate: "I'm there."

Darcy and Mike spent the rest of the afternoon zipping down the hill and struggling back up it. Whenever they wiped out, they rolled in the snow and laughed. Once, they engaged in a brutal snowball fight which ended with Darcy getting a frosty facial.

The setting sun cast long blue shadows across the snowy field. Mike and Darcy hauled the sled to the top of the hill for the last time and called it a day. They were too tired for another trip. Before they returned to the parking lot, Darcy plopped down in the snow on her back. "Hey, watch this." She swung her arms up and down and swished her legs out and in.

"What are you doing?" Mike looked at her like maybe she had landed on her head during one of their falls.

"Making a snow angel," Darcy said matter-of-factly. "Don't you want to make one?"

"I don't think so." Mike took Darcy's hands, pulled her up, and helped her brush off the snow. He put both hands on her shoulders and touched his forehead to hers. "You're angel enough for me."

Back in Aunt Rosie's drive, Mike leaned across the seat and put his hand behind Darcy's neck. "Thank you for the best Christmas gift ever." He brought his face close to hers. "The sled is fantastic," he whispered, "but the best part was spending the afternoon with you."

A light flashed on, and Aunt Rosie appeared on the porch. "Y'all are gonna freeze to death out there," she called. "Come on in and test my coconut cake. I need to make sure it's fit to eat."

Mike and Darcy glanced wistfully at each other. They eased the sled from the back seat and went into the house.

"Look at you two," Aunt Rosie scolded. "You must be near frozen." She handed each of them a mug of hot chocolate and a huge piece of cake.

Darcy had never cared much for coconut, but she took a bite of Aunt Rosie's cake to be polite. The sweet confection melted in her mouth. She had never tasted anything so light and delicate.

"Aunt Rosie," she said with her mouth full, "this is the best cake I ever ate. What's your secret? My mom's coconut cake never tastes like this."

Aunt Rosie lowered her eyes and smiled. "Oh, honey, there's no secret. Tell your mom to be sure and use lots and lots of coconut—Angel Flake."

It was dark by the time Mike and Darcy finished their snack and walked to Darcy's car. Mike helped Darcy put up the top. Then he opened the door, and she slipped behind the wheel.

Mike closed the door and sat back on his heels so that his face was at window level. "Thanks again for the sled. I hope snow stays on the ground all winter, so we can go sledding every day."

"You're welcome, and I hope it does, too." Darcy turned her face toward him.

He reached through the car window and adjusted her stocking hat over her ears. "Call you tomorrow?"

"Looking forward to it."

Darcy started the engine and backed out of the drive. Before she drove away, she turned her head to give Mike one last wave. She squinted then blinked several times. Mike stood on the porch waving, the light from the moon forming a perfect nimbus around his head.

CHAPTER TWENTY-FOUR

Every year Darcy's mom and dad gave her the usual gifts of clothes and jewelry, but there was always one special surprise. On Christmas Day, Darcy tore off the wrapping of a large box and unveiled a… laptop?

She tried to hide her disappointment. "Gee, thanks. I never expected this."

"I know it's not a very glamorous gift," her dad said, "but I think you'll find it useful at college."

"Oh, I know I will. It's…great. Thank you."

Her parents weren't fooling her. This gift was a hint. She still hadn't chosen a college, and although they hadn't said anything, her parents' concern was obvious and understandable. Darcy never waited until the last minute on any decision as important as this. But she couldn't tell them she would pick a college as soon as Mike did.

That afternoon, she drove to Aunt Rosie's , the worry of choosing a college—spurred by the laptop—nagging at her. Her parents would argue that basing her choice on Mike's decision was crazy. But Darcy would never be happy anywhere separated from Mike.

This led to another disturbing thought: Did Mike feel the same about her? There were times when she could swear he did. When she closely examined the facts, though, there was little concrete evidence. She knew he liked her a lot, but *like* didn't equal *love*. He'd never said the word *love*, and he had never even kissed her. Not a real kiss. There'd been that one on the hand in the diner. And the day they went sledding he was right on the verge of it when they were so inconveniently interrupted by Aunt Rosie. But there had never been an arms-embracing, on-the-lips, pulse-raising, breath-stopping kiss.

Well, one step at a time. Darcy couldn't make Mike love her. But the kissing problem would be solved before this day was over.

Thinking of the kiss lifted Darcy's spirits. She hummed "Jingle Bells" as she drove the rest of the way for a quiet dinner with Mike, Aunt Rosie, and maybe a few relatives.

When she arrived, cars lined both sides of the dirt road leading to Aunt Rosie's and were parked every which way in the yard. Darcy zigzagged through the impromptu parking lot and made her way to the front porch. Bells on a wreath jingled when Mike opened the door.

Darcy stepped into the living room and looked around. Wall-to-wall people mingled and greeted each other. "You and Aunt Rosie and a couple of relatives, huh?"

Mike helped Darcy with her coat. "I promise I had no idea."

Aunt Rosie hurried toward Darcy with open arms. With her silver hair and red checkered apron, she resembled a sweet but frazzled Mrs. Claus. "Oh, honey, I'm so glad you came." She embraced Darcy in her plump arms. "Don't let this big ol' crowd scare you. If someone comes up and gives you a bear hug, don't think a thing about it. They probably think you're kin."

Darcy returned the hug. "Merry Christmas," she said, then nodded toward the dining room table. "I see you've been busy. I'm going to sample some of everything."

"Well now, that sounds like a good plan, but save room for dessert. And be sure to try the divinity." Aunt Rosie's eyes twinkled. "It's my specialty."

Aunt Rosie excused herself and hurried back to the kitchen. As she bustled away, she worried aloud. "I sure hope there's enough."

Mike and Darcy looked at each other and burst out laughing. Food covered every square inch of the huge dining room table and overflowed onto the kitchen table and countertops.

Mike introduced Darcy to the crowd of people who packed the old house. Everyone greeted Darcy as if she were a long-time friend. She liked them instantly but couldn't help noticing what an odd assortment they were. In one corner a beautiful, brown-eyed woman of about thirty talked in Spanish to a stooped, wrinkled little man with thinning hair and fading blue eyes. Across the room, a dark-skinned gentleman, impeccably groomed and wearing an expensive suit, engaged in an earnest conversation with a pierced and tattooed teenager dressed from head to toe in black. In yet another group, she noticed a slender lady with olive skin and almond-shaped eyes and a woman with the weathered and ragged appearance of the homeless. In a language Darcy didn't recognize, they spoke with a couple who reminded her of the farmer and wife in *American Gothic*. Running and laughing in and out among the adults were several children, ranging in ages from about four to adolescence. The only thing any of the guests seemed to have in common was their joy at being together to celebrate the season.

During a lull in the introductions, Darcy whispered to Mike, "Surely these aren't all Aunt Rosie's relatives. These people can't possibly be members of the same family."

Mike placed her hand in the crook of his arm and covered it with his. "You'd be surprised," he said.

A handsome, middle-aged man with snow-white hair said a blessing, then Mike and Darcy joined the rest of the guests in heaping their plates. They looked around for a place to sit but didn't find an unoccupied space anywhere on the first floor. Finally, they sat down on the stairs and attacked their food.

Thirty minutes later, they moaned and swore they would never eat another bite. Mike took their plates to the kitchen and re-joined Darcy on the stairs. The two of them lapsed into a stupor as someone in the living room put a record on Aunt Rosie's old phonograph. Strains of Handel's *Messiah* drifted up the staircase. Through the scratches and white noise, the classic oratorio filled the listeners with hope and inspiration.

When the opening chords of the "Hallelujah Chorus" were struck, Darcy turned to Mike. "This is my absolute favorite Christmas song," she said. Mike agreed and joined her as she sang along with the rousing finale.

When the chorus ended, they laughed at their off-key notes and their confusion with the overlapping *hallelujahs*. Then Mike grew serious. "Why is this your favorite carol?" he asked.

Darcy had to think. She had loved this music from the first time she heard it, but she never thought about why. "I think because...because I not only can hear, but I can *feel* the composer's joy over what he's celebrating," she said at last. "It's like all those crazy, jumbled *hallelujah's* come tumbling out of him in some uncontrolled fit of excitement. He doesn't know how to express his emotions in specific words, so he repeats 'Hallelujah' over and over."

When she finished talking, Mike sat staring at her with a look somewhere between disbelief and astonishment. Oh, great, Darcy thought. Now he thinks I'm a complete nutcase. But before she could offer any explanations to the contrary, Mike stood. Without a word, he took her hand and led her to the landing at the top of the stairs. He opened the door to his small bedroom and walked over to an old bureau.

Darcy stood in the doorway and peered into the room. She realized this was not Mike's permanent residence, but the sparse furnishings and lack of belongings startled her. There were no posters, no trophies, no suggestions at all of his past or personal life. The only sports equipment was the Flexible Flyer, which was propped in a corner. On a small desk were a few school books. A worn, dog-eared Bible rested on a nightstand beside his bed. Only one picture decorated the room. The senior picture she had given him was taped to the wall above his headboard.

Mike pulled something from the bureau drawer and walked back onto the landing. "I understand about having difficulty putting feelings into words." He took Darcy's hand and placed a light-blue velvet jewelry box in her palm.

"I brought this from home," he said. "I got it when I went away at Thanksgiving. I don't know exactly how to say it, but I want you to know how special you are. When I came to Easton I never expected to find someone like you...I'm so thankful I did."

Darcy's hands shook as she opened the box. Inside was a delicate silver bracelet with a single charm, an intricately carved star. No diamond or jewel adorned it, yet it glowed with a luster that seemed to come from within. It perfectly reflected the glow in her heart.

"Mike, it's beautiful. So unusual. I love it."

She gave the bracelet to Mike and held out her hand, palm up, for him to put it on her wrist. With his head bent, he fumbled with the clasp. When he finally managed to get it fastened, he took her hand in his and pressed her palm against his face. Then he embraced her in his arms. He kissed her tenderly on the forehead and then on the lips. Darcy's pulse raced, and she could hardly catch her breath.

That evening, with the kitchen cleaned and the guests gone,

Darcy stood on the porch with Aunt Rosie and Mike. "Thank you for a wonderful Christmas," she said and gave Aunt Rosie a parting hug. "I enjoyed meeting your, uh…family. The food was delicious, and your divinity—heavenly."

"Thank you, dear. I'm so glad you could join us. You come again soon." Aunt Rosie dabbed at her eyes. "Oh, I'm such an old softie. Christmas makes me so emotional." She turned and hurried inside.

Arm in arm, Mike and Darcy strolled to her car.

"You'll think I'm crazy for asking this," she said, "but will you help me put Bee's top down?"

"Are you sure? It's freezing out here."

"I know, but it's a clear night, and I want to see the stars." She tilted her head back and inhaled deeply. "Besides, the cool air feels good."

Mike shook his head at the insane request, but he helped Darcy lower the top of the convertible. When she got behind the wheel, he leaned over and gave her a quick kiss. "Good night. Be careful going home. Call you tomorrow." He stood in the yard and watched Darcy and Bee head back down the road.

As she drove home, the angel charm dangled on her wrist, emitting its soft light. Darcy was the happiest she'd ever been in her life. She loved the bracelet, she loved Mike, and she had indeed remedied that kissing problem.

Hal-le-eh-lu-jah!

CHAPTER TWENTY-FIVE

After basketball practice, Mike stood in front of Coach Hudson's desk, with a sense of dread. He knew what the coach was going to ask, and Mike had been avoiding the issue.

"Mike," the coach said, "I've been getting a lot of calls lately. Some of the best basketball colleges in the country are interested in you. Any ideas about where you'd like to go?"

Rather than answer right away, Mike let his thoughts drift back to the recent holidays. He and Darcy had spent as much time as they could together—sometimes with friends, sometimes just the two of them. But the blissful time had passed as quickly as a New Year's Eve countdown, and now they were once again caught up in their hectic schedules.

Basketball consumed most of Mike's waking hours. Easton High's season was the most successful in fifteen years with a win-loss record of twenty-three/two. All the polls ranked Easton as number one in the state, and the team's appearance at the state tournament seemed certain. The fans' hopes of a championship placed tremendous pressure on Mike. He longed for the stress-free pace of the holidays.

Today in response to Coach Hudson's question, Mike groaned inwardly. The coach's look of expectancy indicated he thought he was telling Mike exciting news. But Mike had been avoiding calls from college scouts and recruiters for the past two months. Now he fumbled for an answer. "No, sir,...right now I don't know where I want to play, and I...uh...don't want to think about it."

Why not?" Coach Hudson rubbed his bald head. "You surely know every high school basketball player in the nation would be jumping at opportunities like these. Heh, heh, no pun intended."

Mike ducked his head and shuffled his weight from side to side. "Well, uh, I love playing for Easton. And now that we have a good shot at the playoffs, I want to concentrate on playing my best high school ball and help Easton win state."

Coach Hudson beamed like a proud father as Mike continued. "As soon as the season's over, I'll think about college plans. Right now, though, I want to take care of the business at hand."

The coach slapped Mike on the back and congratulated him on his mature thinking and dedication to the team.

Mike fought back feelings of guilt as he exited Coach Hudson's office. He couldn't believe the coach had bought that line of bull. Worse than that, he couldn't believe he'd said it. But at this point, he couldn't handle any more hassle. And he couldn't tell Coach Hudson, the recruiters, or anyone else he wasn't interested in any college offers. He had no intention of going to college. Ever.

That afternoon, he squatted in the school parking lot unchaining his bike from a signpost near the curb. A thirty mile-an-hour wind from the north made the 33^0 temperature seem more like 20^0. His fingers were numb as he worked the combination on the lock. A car roared up beside him and stopped.

"It's kind of cold to be riding a bike." Tiffin leaned out the car window and gave him a well-rehearsed smile. "Put it in the back, and I'll give you a lift."

Mike was in no mood to deal with Tiffin today. In the first place, she tended to emotionally drain a person, and he was already dragging from a grueling practice. Secondly, unless she was facing something life-threatening, he wanted to avoid her for Darcy's sake. Since his and Darcy's talk at the diner, Darcy hadn't said one word about Tiffin, and he appreciated her understanding. He didn't want to cause Darcy concern if the situation didn't require it. Today—as far as he could tell—it didn't.

"Thanks," he said, still working at the combination, "but I want to ride my bike. Maybe the cold air will energize me."

The corners of Tiffin's mouth drooped, and her eyes misted over. "Please, Mike. I need to talk to you. Can't we go somewhere for a little while?"

In the booth at Ted's, Mike shifted uneasily. He had suggested Ted's because there was little chance of Tiffin and him being seen by anyone who knew them. This meeting was entirely innocent—on his part anyway—but he wasn't sure how Darcy would react if she learned about it.

Maybe there was no need for concern. He had seen a definite shift in Darcy's attitude over the past few weeks. There had been times when she made attempts to be friendly to Tiffin. Of course, Tiffin's responses ranged between sarcasm and flat-out rudeness, but still Darcy kept trying.

"I'm sorry to keep bothering you," Tiffin said, "but there's no one else I can talk to. Reese is getting worse. He hasn't pushed or shoved me lately, but he threatens me. He says stuff like 'You're my property...I can do anything I want to you.' He doesn't want me to hang out with my girlfriends anymore, and the other night he kicked a dent in the fender of my car."

Mike listened to Tiffin's words with rising alarm. He leaned in close to her face and spoke firmly. "Listen to me. You *have* to do something. Report him to the police. Get a restraining order. This guy is out of control. It's only a matter of time before he does real harm."

"I don't know." She looked down and picked at her plastic fingernails. "Sometimes he scares me. But in the next minute he can be kind of sweet. He tells me he loves me and begs me to forgive him. Says he can't live without me. I don't want to get him into any serious trouble."

Mike's jaw ached as it tightened. His anger at Reese and his frustration with Tiffin had pushed him to the edge of his patience. He had to think of a way to get through to her. "Tiffin," he said, sounding like an angry parent. "You have just given a textbook description of an abuser." He emphasized every word. "Get help. Tell your mother. Tell—"

"Hah! That'll be a big help." Tiffin slammed back in the booth with her arms folded across her chest. She sulked for a few seconds and avoided his disapproving stare. Then, her words tinged with bitterness, she began her explanation. "Okay, true confession. You want to know why I don't report Reese? Because my mother would throw me out. If that shocks you, let me fill you in on some family history."

She had to go way back in order for the story to make sense. "My mother's father was a shiftless, abusive man. Dodie figured marriage was her only ticket out of the hell she called home, so at seventeen she married Hal Griffith. I was born seven months later." She gave Mike a defiant look. "My dad was a successful insurance salesman who cared about appearances. So when I was two years old, he decided he had married beneath him and divorced my mother." She gave a harsh laugh. "Apparently he decided to divorce me, too. I think the only time he ever thinks about me is when he writes his child support checks."

"Tiffin, I'm sorry. I—"

"Wait, the story is just getting good." Tiffin stared straight at Mike. "After my dad, Dodie had several husbands or boyfriends. With the husbands, times were good. There were big houses, swimming pools, cool clothes and vacations. The boyfriends left Dodie with unpaid bills and calls from bill collectors. The only way get out of debt was to marry again. But lately the husbands are becoming harder to find."

"It must have been tough for you," Mike said. "Did your mom ever consider going back to school or training for a career?"

"She took some modeling classes. And one time she started an on-line course in interior decorating, but she never finished it." Tiffin shrugged. "I guess she tried hard, but nothing ever seemed to work out for her."

As far as Mike could determine from Tiffin's story, Doris had learned two skills: how to spend money and how to trap a man. And those were the lessons she passed on to her daughter. Now Tiffin was the one caught in the trap.

"Dodie's only hope, these days," Tiffin continued, "for me and for her—is for me to marry well. Right now, Reese is the best prospect for fulfilling that hope." Her voice caught. Her shoulders sagged and her lips trembled. "*Reese.* Can you imagine? Whenever I complain about his violent temper or threats, Dodie gets mad and says, 'Grow up, Tiffin. No man is perfect.'"

Tiffin stared at her hands in her lap. Mike hadn't seen her this forlorn and dejected since the night he rescued her from Reese at the basketball game. He'd already known about her horrible home life and the way her mother was trying to unload her on Reese. But hearing her tell the story made it more tragic. At a time when other young women were making choices about colleges, sororities, and career paths, it must have seemed to Tiffin she had only one path before her—a dead-end one.

"Tiffin, there are places to get help," Mike said. "Agencies, school counselors. What about your church?"

Tiffin looked up. Her lip curled, and she frowned as if Mike had suggested she seek help at a halfway house for addicts. "I haven't been to church since I was four years old," she said. "We moved to a little hick town somewhere in western Oklahoma to live with Dodie's new boyfriend. One day, the neighbor next door asked me if I wanted to go to church with her. Dodie thought she was a busybody but made me go with her to get me out of the house for a while."

Tiffin rested her chin in her hand. A wistful expression came to her eyes, and a smile played around the corners of her lips. "I actually enjoyed the Sunday school class for the little kids. We colored and sang and had juice and cookies. The ladies there were nice, and I liked the stories they told about God and Jesus. That was the first time in my life I felt like someone truly loved me or cared what happened to me.

"But we didn't stay there long. Dodie broke up with her boyfriend after a few weeks, and we came back to Easton." The look of disgust returned to Tiffin's face as she peered down at the table. "I haven't thought about God in a long time, and I'm pretty sure He's forgotten about me."

Mike's heart ached for Tiffin. He sensed she had come to the place to hear what he had wanted to tell her for a long time: *God loved her. He knew about her problems and wanted to help her.*

He reached across the table and lightly grasped Tiffin's forearm. As soon as he did, she raised her eyes to meet his.

"Oh, Mike," she said softly. "I feel the same way about you." She clutched his hand in both of hers and pressed it to her cheek. Her eyes were round and glistening, and her smile beamed with hope.

Her face told Mike he had made a terrible mistake. Tiffin was desperate. She would grasp at anything. She had mistaken a gesture of compassion for an act of romantic love.

CHAPTER TWENTY-SIX

Mike jerked his hand away. "Tiffin...I don't—"

She reached across the table and placed two fingers on Mike's lips. "Shh. Don't say a thing. I completely understand."

No, you don't. You don't understand at all. But Mike couldn't find the words to tell Tiffin how wrong she was. Even if he could, he didn't know how to handle the scene she was sure to create. He stood and put some money on the table for the bill. Then he made a quick retreat from the diner and unloaded his bike from Tiffin's car.

Mike hunched his shoulders against the brutal headwind and pedaled furiously toward home. How could he have been so stupid? To mislead someone in Tiffin's state of mind was more than careless—it was cruel. Had he completely forgotten all his training?

Another thought nagged at him. What if Darcy found out? What if she heard Tiffin's twisted version of this entire incident? Would she understand?

Panic seized Mike. With Tiffin involved, sooner or later Darcy would hear her version of the story. And Darcy would *not* understand.

Days later, Mike brainstormed for a way to handle the predicament with Tiffin as he cleaned out a stall in Aunt Rosie's barn. The sound of an engine and the crunch of gravel in the driveway interrupted his thoughts. Looking across the barnyard, he saw Reese, Lance and Tucker climb from Reese's truck. They mounted the steps to the farmhouse porch and banged on the door.

Beside Mike, a massive Rottweiler growled from deep in his barreled chest. "Easy, boy," he said and patted his head. "Aunt Rosie can handle this."

"Well, if it isn't the nice young men I met at the market," he heard Aunt Rosie say. "What a pleasant surprise!" She stepped out on the porch. "Can I help you?"

"We're looking for Mike," Reese said.

"Oh, my. I'm so sorry, but he's not here right now."

"Yeah? When'll he be back?"

"Well, I'm not sure. He's doing some errands for me. Can I give him a message?"

Reese turned to the other two and smirked. Lance and Tucker guffawed and elbowed each other like they were in on some big joke.

"Yeah. When he gets back, tell him Reese was lookin' for him. Tell him I know all about him and Tiffin meeting at Ted's. If he knows what's good for him, he'd better stop pokin' his nose where it don't belong."

Aunt Rosie was all sympathy and concern. "I'll be sure and give him the message, Reese. He'll be sorry he missed you. I'm sure he'd be eager to clear up this misunderstanding."

Halfway back to Reese's truck, Tucker stopped. "Hey, Reese," he said. He nodded at the side of the house. "There's his bike."

Reese's eyes narrowed. "Sure 'nough. And the old lady's car is here."

"So that means choirboy is around here somewhere." Tucker's face broke into a stupid grin.

The boys headed toward the back of the house.

In the barn, the dog's growl grew more menacing. "Patience," Mike said.

The boys circled the house and stopped in the front yard. Then they spotted the barn and started walking toward it, shoulder to shoulder, their hands balled into fists.

When they were ten feet away, Mike gave the command. The Rottweiler stormed from the barn like a raging bull. Saliva flew from his bared teeth and vicious snarls gurgled in his throat.

Reese, Lance and Tucker looked up to see one-hundred-twenty pounds of animal wrath thundering at them. Their screams could be heard in the next county as they turned and ran as if the devil himself were chasing them. They reached the truck and dived for safety, narrowly escaping the dog's vise-like jaws. Dirt flew as the truck spun out of the drive.

118

Mike stopped laughing long enough to whistle and call the dog. On hearing the signal, the dog returned, panting with fatigue but clearly pleased with himself.

"Good boy!" Mike kneeled down and rubbed the dog behind the ears. "You're not mean , are you, Diablo? You just don't like people poking their noses where they don't belong."

* * * *

Col. Michael contacted Mike that evening. "Good news, Mike! Mission completed. You can return home."

Mike wasn't sure he understood. The mission couldn't be over. "Are you certain, sir?"

In agitation, Col. Michael asked, "Are you questioning orders?" Then he spoke with a hint of compassion. "I know it's difficult to pull up stakes at a moment's notice, but we have to trust those in command. They see the overall picture more clearly than we do."

Mike already knew this. Service life had proven the truth of these words time and again. Still, he wasn't ready to leave. He bargained for a little more time.

* * * *

Weeks passed with no indication Darcy had found out about Mike's meeting with Tiffin. This puzzled Mike. If Reese knew about it, it couldn't be a secret. But Tiffin must have been waiting for the right time to share her version of the story with Darcy—a time when it would do the most damage.

Tiffin hadn't said anything, but she had become bolder in her behavior toward Mike. Whenever Reese wasn't around, Tiffin took advantage of his absence. She would touch Mike in some affectionate way, snuggle against him in the hall, end each conversation with a hug and "Love you." She slipped notes taped through the vents of his locker that told him how much he meant to her. No dodging or disinterest on his part discouraged her.

Ironically, Mike's best defense was Reese. Tiffin had to handle her fantasized romance carefully. If Reese found out the way she was behaving toward Mike, there was no telling what he would do to her.

Mike considered explaining everything to Darcy himself, but that would look like damage control—like he was trying to tell his version first. So in spite of—or perhaps because of—his feelings for Darcy, he went through these days existing in a snow-globe world. Everything appeared perfect and serene. But with one slight shake from Tiffin, he would find himself in the middle of a whirling storm.

CHAPTER TWENTY-SEVEN

Mike was dreading another event—Valentine's Day. Not a male on the face of the earth could possibly look forward to that day. He knew the origin of the legend—St. Valentine and all that—but he was certain greeting card companies and florists had promoted the day to its current overblown status. The pressure was getting to him.

He stood in the stationery aisle of the drugstore and read one stupid card after another. He picked up a Victorian valentine with a picture of a chubby, baby-faced cherub, toting a bow and arrow. *Ridiculous.* Whoever dreamed up such a creature? A contemporary card was worse. On the front a lecherous-looking chimpanzee leered at the reader. The message inside: "Hey, Valentine, Let's monkey around!" *Huh?* Was that supposed to be romantic? He slapped the card back on the shelf and stomped out of the store.

Darcy hadn't made an issue over Valentine's Day. She wasn't dropping hints left and right or making outright demands like some girls he'd overheard. But after missing her birthday and after the fantastic gift she'd given him for Christmas, he had to do something equally fantastic for her.

After much tortured deliberation and some advice from Aunt Rosie, he came up with a plan. Darcy had shared a special place with him for Christmas. He would do the same for her for Valentine's.

On February 13, he called Darcy. "What are your plans for tomorrow evening?"

"Well," she said, drawing out the word, "I had made plans to go out with Michael Nerdly. But at the last minute, he decided to re-organize his stamp collection, so those plans have been cancelled. Those wild and crazy philatelists—you never know what they'll do next. Do you have anything in mind?"

"Sure do. I'll pick you up at 6:45. Dress warm!"

"Where are we—" Darcy began, but before she could finish, Mike hung up.

* * * *

The evening of February 14, Darcy stood in her bedroom applying Chapstick® to her lips when she heard her doorbell ring. She checked her phone. *6:40.* Ever punctual, Mike was right on time.

"Come in, Mike," she heard her dad say. Then she heard the two exchange information about the weather and Easton High's basketball season.

Darcy came down the stairs, and Mike glanced at his watch. "We'll have to hurry. I've made reservations."

She looked down at her insulated hiking boots, jeans, and ski parka, then raised a fleece-lined mitten in front of Mike's face. "I've got more padding than the Pillsbury Doughboy and we're going to a place that requires reservations? Maybe I'd better change."

Mike took her hand and pulled her out the door. "You're perfect," he said. "Let's go."

Chet called out last minute instructions to drive carefully as Darcy and Mike walked to the car. The temperature was barely above freezing, but there was no wind. The air was crisp and energizing, and there wasn't a trace of clouds in the cobalt sky.

Mike had parked Aunt Rosie's immaculate 1964 Oldsmobile Jetstar 88 at the curb. "My gosh!" Darcy exclaimed as she lowered herself onto the front seat of the ancient vehicle. "I've seen this car in Aunt Rosie's drive, but I never realized how huge it is inside."

Mike cranked up the V8 engine and pulled away from the curb. "I know, it's a tank. And it only gets about five miles to the gallon. But I figure, what the heck? It's not every day we get to ride in a car that can double as a gymnasium."

Then he grinned. "There's another great feature about these old cars—bench seats. Slide over here and let's take advantage of that option."

Darcy scooted across the seat. She pitied the man who invented bucket seats and consoles. He must have never had a girlfriend.

Mike drove back toward Aunt Rosie's, but about a mile before they got to her house, he turned right and took off across a vacant field.

"Where are we going?" Darcy asked. From the teeth-rattling ride, she could tell there wasn't so much as a dirt road here.

Mike ignored the question.

The old car handled the bumpy route like an all-terrain vehicle. Darcy would have been alarmed with any other guy. But she trusted Mike completely. She looked down at her hand in her lap. The star charm had slipped out from under her mitten, and in the darkness of the car it emitted its mysterious glow. She fingered it gently and snuggled close to Mike, ready to enjoy the adventure.

After a few hundred feet, Mike turned again and cut behind a grove of trees. Then, at the top of a hill seemingly miles from nowhere, he stopped the car.

"We're here," he announced and turned off the engine. He helped Darcy from the car and reached in the back to retrieve a picnic basket. He switched on a flashlight, then turned to Darcy and bowed. "Madam, may I show you to your table?" He offered her his arm.

Darcy looked around. They were in the middle of a field, but in the distance a huge boulder about six feet high and flat on top jutted from the ground. The rock looked out of place…like it had dropped from the sky into this otherwise gently rolling landscape. She clung to Mike's arm as he led her to it.

Mike and Darcy climbed on top of the rock. Mike set the basket down and extinguished the light. Looking at the sky, he turned slowly in a circle. Then he stood behind Darcy and wrapped his arms around her. He lowered his lips to her ear. "Look up. Isn't this fantastic?" he whispered.

Darcy did as he instructed and was transfixed by the sight. She had never seen so many stars. On this cloudless night, miles from any city lights, the sky was ablaze. Some stars shone brightly, some formed a milky haze. Occasionally, one shot across the sky, a luminous tail attached to it.

"I can't believe it," Darcy said in a hush. "All this beauty exists only a few miles from where I've lived all my life, and I didn't know it. How did you find this place?"

Mike explained he discovered it by accident. The day his truck cratered, he had been forced to take an unplanned detour. This is where he ended up. "It's so peaceful," he said. "I know it sounds ridiculous, but I feel like I can connect with my dad up here. I come here and tell him my problems, and he helps me...lets me know what I should do. I come here when I need to sort things out." Mike paused, and then said, "I love this place, and I wanted to share it with you."

The two stood in silence for a long while, drinking in the star-studded, velvet night. Then, abruptly changing the mood, Mike reached for the basket. "All this beauty is making me hungry. Let's eat." He opened the basket, pulled out a table cloth, and spread it across the flat surface of the rock.

"The man who thinks of everything," Darcy said.

He brought out two candlesticks, candleholders, and matches. "I have to give Aunt Rosie credit for these," he said as he lit the candles. "She thought they would be much more romantic than a flashlight."

Mike continued to lay out a meal of cheese, fruit, and Aunt Rosie's homemade bread. "And this," he said, "is Aunt Rosie's valentine to both of us." He lifted an angel food cake with strawberry icing from the basket.

Darcy watched with astonishment as he continued to pull food out of the basket. How had he ever managed to pack so much into such a small container? Then Mike brought out two stemmed glasses and a chilled bottle with a foil wrapper on the top. She raised her eyebrows.

Mike winked and rotated the bottle to reveal the label— Sparkling Grape Juice. "Like you said, the man who thinks of everything."

They finished their meal and sat side by side on the edge of the rock, letting their legs dangle over. Mike put his arm around Darcy. She leaned her head against him, and they counted shooting stars, all the time *oohing* and *aahing* at the celestial light show.

"I have to admit," Mike said, "this view makes 'beyond the farthest star' a tempting place. Do you still want to go there? "

"That depends," Darcy said.

"On what?"

"On whether you're going with me."

He gave her shoulders a squeeze. "No, unfortunately, I'm not going with you on this trip."

"Okay, then, maybe I won't go to the *farthest* star. Maybe I'll go to Proxima Centauri, instead."

"Very impressive," Mike said. "I see you paid attention in science class. Why would you go there?"

"Because Proxima Centauri is the closest star to the earth other than the sun, and no way am I going there—Oklahoma gets plenty hot enough for me. And if you're not going with me, I don't want to be any farther away than necessary."

He swallowed. "Do you know how long it would take you to get there?"

"I have no idea. This is where I stopped listening in science class."

"Well, lucky for you I didn't." Mike shifted into a teacher mode. "If you went to Proxima Centauri on the fastest manned vehicle we have at the moment, your estimated time of arrival would be 32,000 years from now. And that's not including pit stops."

"I've changed my mind then. I'm not going at all." Darcy pressed her mouth into a determined line.

"Why not?"

"Because the round trip would take 64,000 years—I did listen in math class. That's too long to be away from you. That's an eternity. And I don't want to be separated from you for a single day."

Mike finally spoke. "I don't want to be away from you, either. But right now I can't promise I will always be around." His breath condensed on the cold night air as he exhaled. "You must have a million questions about me—who I am, where I came from, what my future plans are. I'm sorry I can't answer those questions now. I will some day, but I have a few things to work out. For now, I can only ask you to trust me. I know that's asking a lot, but it's all I can do."

Darcy sat silently, thinking. She did have a million questions about him. In the midst of all those questions, though, there was one certainty. She loved Mike. It was not a schoolgirl crush or infatuation or teenage hormones working overtime. It was love.

"I'd never ask you to tell me anything you can't or don't want to," she said. "I don't need your life history to know the person you are." She laughed. "And if I didn't trust you, I wouldn't be out here in the middle of nowhere with you."

Mike removed his arm from around Darcy's shoulders and took both her hands in his. "What if I change my answer? If I went on this trip with you, would you go? Would you trust me enough to go that far away with me?"

She sat as still as a statue, hardly daring to breathe. For months she had fantasized about a moment like this. She had imagined Mike's words and thought about her answers. Now she looked straight into his eyes and spoke with no hesitation. "I would go with you beyond the farthest star."

Over the next two weeks, Darcy gave detailed accounts of Valentine's night to Megan, Susan, Lacey, and anyone else who would listen. Nothing "official" had been announced, but around school everyone understood she and Mike were a couple. Darcy raced through her busy, happy days without the slightest warning of the dangerous storm brewing on the horizon.

CHAPTER TWENTY-EIGHT

March Madness—the high school version—dominated the thoughts of every student at Easton High. Tennis officially began the first day of March, but the sport foremost on Darcy's mind was basketball. At every home game, she joined the throngs who packed the school gym.

During the week of the state playoffs, as Easton battled its way to the finals, another rivalry was building. A warm front from the south ushered spring-like conditions into the state. The mild daytime temperatures coaxed out the blooms on daffodils, redbuds, and pear trees. Billowy clouds sailed in a peaceful sea of blue sky. But an obstinate cold front was shoving its way down from the north. Whenever and wherever the rival fronts collided, violent weather would erupt.

On the Saturday morning of the final game, local weather stations issued a tornado watch. But Oklahomans, accustomed to life in Tornado Alley, would never allow anything less than an actual tornado to spoil a major sporting event.

In the afternoon, thousands poured into State Fair Arena, "The Big House," in Oklahoma City. The Easton Eagles were challenging the defending state champs, the Bradleyville Tigers.

Inside the huge arena, Mike sat on the bench, his heart racing. He scanned the crowd for Darcy and finally located her. When he caught her eye, she shouted her customary rallying cry of "Go, Mike!" and raised her hand to form a victory sign. He was ready to play.

The game against Bradleyville proved to be of championship caliber down to the final buzzer. The Tigers fought hard to defend their title, but Easton claimed the victory. Bedlam broke out in the arena. With the rest of the Easton fans, Darcy raced to the gym floor, straight into

Mike's arms.

The Booster Club had been sure of an Eagle win. They were also confident in their ability to defy nature. A celebration in Easton had been planned for after the game. Everyone would gather in the school parking lot for a bonfire, victory speeches, and a dance.

Mike had to shower and then ride to the party on the team bus. He and Darcy made plans to meet by the school's flagpole, away from the frenzy in the parking lot.

"I probably won't be able to get near you," Darcy teased. "I'll need a bulldozer to get through all your adoring fans." She laughed when she saw Mike blush.

* * * *

By the time Darcy arrived at school, dark clouds blocked out the evening sun, and wind gusts threatened to dislodge the victory banner from the light poles. But the celebrating was underway. Hundreds of students crowded the roped-off section of the parking lot shouting, "We're Number One!" Streamers and balloons flapped in the wind. The band played the school fight song over and over with unflagging enthusiasm. When the team showed up, the players would be introduced on a makeshift stage in the middle of the lot. The coach would give the victory speech, then the dancing would begin and last late into the night.

With Megan and Chad, Darcy plowed her way through the crowd to join the rest of their friends. They all gabbed excitedly while they waited for the team to arrive. Before the activities started, Darcy excused herself to go to the ladies room inside the school foyer.

* * * *

Tiffin glared at Darcy from across the parking lot. She had seen Darcy throw herself at Mike after the game. Once again, jealousy consumed her. Why should Darcy be sharing this moment with him? Mike cared more for her than he did for Darcy. He made it perfectly clear that night at Ted's.

Tiffin saw Darcy walking toward the restroom. She grabbed Angie's arm. "Come with me," she said and pulled her friend in that direction.

"Oh, darn!" Tiffin stopped and bent down. She picked up a cheap silver bracelet with a rhinestone charm, the one she'd been wearing ever since she'd spied Darcy's. "This clasp is always coming undone." She handed the bracelet to Angie, who re-fastened it on Tiffin's wrist.

The two entered the restroom, and Tiffin checked under the stalls to be sure Darcy was in one. Then she stood in front of a mirror and applied mascara with a heavy hand. She spoke to Angie more loudly than necessary. "Yeah, me and Mike have become very—I mean, *very*—close over the past few weeks. He's been so sweet to help me with some personal problems, and, well, I guess he finally realized how much he cares for me."

Angie raised a skeptical eyebrow and faced Tiffin. "Are you talking about Mike as in Mike Albright?"

"Yes!" Tiffin almost shouted and her face lit up.

"Girl, you're hallucinating." Angie peered in the mirror and checked her teeth. "Everyone in school knows Mike and Darcy are an item. As in *tight*." She held up her hand with her fingers crossed. "Haven't you seen them at school? Always walking together, holding hands, staring into each other's eyes." She opened her mouth and poked her index finger toward her throat. "It's enough to make me gag. But at the same time, it's kind of sweet."

Tiffin ignored Angie and put away the mascara. "Mike's going along with her right now," she said, still speaking loudly. "But we went to Ted's one night, and Mike indicated how much he cares for me."

"Oh, yeah?" Always one to welcome juicy gossip, Angie turned and faced her friend again. "Exactly what did he say?"

Tiffin rummaged through her purse and took out some fruity lip gloss. After applying it, she smacked her lips, holding the tube in mid-air. "Well," she said, "it's not so much what he *said*, but what he *did*." She giggled. "You know…nonverbal communication and all that."

"What about Reese? He thinks you're his personal property. He's not going to take this without a fight."

Tiffin stood erect and stuck out her chin. She tried to sound tough, despite an uncontrolled quiver in her voice. "I know. But like I told you the first day of school, I've been meaning to break off this relationship for a long time. Now I don't have to worry about Reese. Mike won't let him hurt me."

Tiffin turned toward the stall and raised her volume another notch. "I feel so sorry for Darcy. This will break her heart. I'm sure Mike's the only boyfriend she's ever had."

She faced the mirror again, smeared on another layer of gloss, and plopped the tube back into her purse. She checked her make-up one last time and left the restroom with Angie.

With Darcy out of the way, she could deal with Reese.

CHAPTER TWENTY-NINE

Tiffin told Angie she'd join her later and walked away to search for Reese. She found him in the parking lot, standing with Lance and Tucker among some parked cars. She stuck out her chest, took a deep breath, and walked toward them. "What are you doing, Reese? Conducting *business*?" she asked sarcastically,

Reese shoved something into his pocket. Lance and Tucker scattered.

"If I am, Tiffin, it's my business, so butt out."

"I'll be glad to." Tiffin put her hands on her hips. Knowing Reese wouldn't hurt her with a crowd so nearby bolstered her courage. "As a matter of fact," she said, "I'm 'butting out' of your life completely. We're through, Reese. I'm breaking up with you."

Reese hooked his thumbs in his pockets and cocked his head. "Yeah, right. I've heard that before. And who do you think you're leaving me for? I hope you don't think that panty-waist jock is interested in you."

Tiffin felt the blood drain from her face.

"That's right, Tiffin. I know about the way you're after him when I'm not around. My sources tell me you're all over him." His lip curled into a cruel grin. "But the last time I looked, he already had a girlfriend. And, believe me, Tiffin, you're not in her league."

She jerked her chin up. "Shut up, Reese. You don't know what you're talking about."

Reese lit a cigarette and took a long drag on it. Then he spoke low and deliberately. "I know this. He ain't gonna trade a pedigree like hers for a mutt like you. She might be a stuck-up ice-princess, but look at her. She's got everything a guy like him would want—looks, style...*brains*.

And then—" he gave a sadistic laugh—"look at you."

Tiffin bit her lip to keep it from trembling while Reese inflicted more injury. "You go on. Run to your choirboy. I'm not gonna stop you. You know why? 'Cause you'll be back." Reese flicked the cigarette to the ground and crushed it beneath his shoe. "Face it, Tiffin. I'm the only kind of guy that'll ever be interested in a girl like you."   Tiffin's face burned, and she blinked back tears as she walked away from Reese. He had hurt her for the last time. She'd find Mike, and she'd be rid of Reese for good.

* * * *

Darcy's head swam as she left the restroom stall and walked to the sink. She looked in the mirror and talked out loud to calm herself. "Only Tiffin could come up with such drivel. No way could Mike be seriously interested in someone like her."

The cool water she splashed on her face didn't squelch the flames of anger raging inside her. "Tiffin was lying. Mike would never be so two-timing."

She ripped a paper towel from the dispenser and dried her face. "She had to be lying. Her lips were moving." Darcy chunked the towel at the trash bin and stomped out of the restroom.

At least she could be relieved about one thing. Tiffin's threats on the first day of school hadn't been directed at her, but at Reese. Okay, so maybe Tiffin was no longer dangerous. But she was still evil.

Outside, roiling thunderheads covered the sky, and the lights in the parking lot sliced through the premature darkness. The wind had increased to gale force, but no one was leaving the party.

The basketball team had been introduced and left the stage. With difficulty, Darcy shoved her way through the crowd. She had to find Mike.

* * * *

Mike leaned against the flagpole, wondering what was keeping Darcy. He started once to look for her but decided to stay put. He would never find her in this mob.   Someone called his name, and with a smile he turned to greet—oh, no...Tiffin.

Tiffin ran toward him with her arms widespread. "Mike! I've been looking everywhere for you!" Her cheerfulness sounded forced.

When she reached him, Tiffin jumped up and wrapped her legs around Mike's waist and her arms around his neck. The impact of her

132

attack nearly knocked him over. She made motions to plant a huge kiss on his mouth, but before she could make contact, he turned his face away. "What are you doing?" he yelled.

He reached behind his neck and grabbed her wrists in an attempt to peel her off. The silver bracelet dropped to the ground.

Tiffin stuck out her lower lip. "Aw, look what you did." She untangled her legs from around him and stooped to retrieve the bracelet. Then she stood up and thrust it into his hand. "Here. Put this back on for me."

She held out her hand, palm up, for him to put the bracelet on her wrist. Mike didn't protest. Anything to get rid of her as soon as possible. With his head bent down, he fumbled with the clasp. As he did, the rhinestone charm reflected the light which shone from the base of the flagpole.

"There," Mike said and closed the clasp. "Now, please—"

Mike looked up to see Darcy. He started to smile, but her stricken look stopped him. What had she seen? He looked at Tiffin. What had Tiffin told her? She spun around and started running. Mike brushed Tiffin aside and chased after her.

"Darcy, wait! Wait!"

She stopped and faced him. Her hair whipped in the wind. A bolt of lightning revealed her anguish. Mike knew Tiffin's storm had struck. A storm which carried the destructive force of a tornado.

"Darcy, please, listen to me. You don't understand."

"Okay, Mike, I'm listening. Explain."

"Darcy...I ...Tiffin was..." Mike hung his head. He couldn't bear to see the heartache he had caused. Where to begin explaining this twisted mess? He looked at her with an unsteady smile and said the only words that came to him. "If you could go—"

"Don't!" Darcy held up her hand as if to physically stop him. "Don't. It hurts too much," she said softly. A tear slid down her cheek. She turned and ran, disappearing into the crowd.

Mike yearned to follow her. But he couldn't. There wasn't time. He headed in the opposite direction, past the flagpole, past Tiffin.

"Mike! Mike, I..."

He heard Tiffin calling to him. But he continued walking, dismissing her with a backward wave of his arm.

* * * *

133

Tiffin stood motionless. Then she swiped at her eyes with the back of her hand. She straightened her shoulders and strutted toward the crowd. When she saw Angie, she asked, "Have you seen Reese?"

＊＊＊＊

Tires screeched as Darcy tore out of the parking lot. She sped toward home. The wind shook the little car, but she was too hurt and angry to be alarmed.

When she reached the unpopulated stretch of road near her house, pain and anger still clawed at her insides. That nightmare scene of Tiffin and Mike seared her memory. How could he have given Tiffin a bracelet like hers? She had trusted Mike. Swallowed all that nonsense about the farthest star. What a line! She couldn't believe how gullible she'd been.

In the darkness, the soft glow of the star charm caught her eye. She had worn this bracelet every day since Mike gave it to her, taking it off only to shower. Once a source of joy, it was now a source of sorrow, a taunting reminder of heartache and betrayal. She ripped the bracelet off her wrist and flung it out the window.

Before the bracelet had time to hit the ground, Darcy slammed on the brakes. She pulled over on the shoulder and rested her forehead on the steering wheel. "What have I done?" she moaned. She backed up, shined the lights where the bracelet must have landed, and bolted from the car.

Her whole body quaked as she searched for the bracelet. "It couldn't have fallen very far. It has to be near—the charm!" She ran back to Bee and turned off the headlights. Surely in this darkness the star's constant glow would reveal the bracelet.

Darcy searched the side of the road for what seemed like hours. Her remorse turned to panic. Had she acted too fast? Perhaps there was an explanation for the scene she had witnessed. What if she'd lost Mike for good?

Darcy prayed. "Please, God, help me find the bracelet." But the bracelet had vanished.

Darcy covered her face with her hands and dropped to the ground. She curled forward, placing her head on her knees. Out here with no one to see or hear her, she wailed, holding nothing back. Even the howling wind didn't drown out her cries. The angry clouds at last released their venom, but she didn't feel the huge, cold drops pelting her body. Hurt, fear, and despair had left her numb. She had lost the bracelet forever. And along with it, she had lost Mike.

* * * *

"Welcome back, Mike! It's wonderful to have you home again."

"Thank you, sir. It's good to see you, too." Mike wanted to return Col. Michael's enthusiasm, but he couldn't cover up his sadness.

"Is something wrong?" Col. Michael asked. "You're usually overjoyed at these homecomings."

"I'm sorry. I am happy to be back...but... part of me thinks I should still be in Easton."

"Oh?"

Mike hesitated, trying to think of a way to explain. "I don't think this was a very good time to leave."

Col. Michael spoke with concern. "We made these plans weeks ago. The mission was essentially over then, but you asked for a few more weeks. Something about a basketball game, wasn't it?"

"Yes, sir." Mike recalled the arrangement. His request to see Easton's basketball season through to the end had been sincere. But more time with Darcy was the real reason he had begged for an extension.

"Is there something you need to tell me?" the colonel asked.

There was nothing he could hide from his senior officer. The two were so close it sometimes seemed as if Col. Michael knew his thoughts before he did. "I guess," Mike said, "the best place to start is at the beginning," and he recounted every detail of his Easton experience, starting with the day he met Darcy.

He told of his attraction to her the first time he saw her. He knew they could have no future, so he tried to stay away from her. But something he couldn't quite explain drew him to her, and ultimately his attraction grew into love. He told how this love had caused both Darcy and Tiffin pain.

"I'm sorry I've made such a mess of this mission," Mike said. "I never thought loving someone could cause so much heartache."

"No need to apologize. You did your best. We can't always control circumstances or choose our feelings." Col. Michael paused before continuing. "If you could decide how things would turn out," he asked, "what would you want to happen?"

"I'd want everyone to be safe. And I'd want Darcy here...with me...always. I know it's selfish, and I know it's impossible. But—being

135

honest with you and with myself—that's what I want."

Col. Michael said nothing for a long while. At last he broke the silence. "A solution doesn't immediately come to mind. Bringing someone here is highly irregular. I'm not sure it's ever been done before. But I'll give your request serious and prayerful thought, and I'll discuss it with my Superior. Maybe we can come up with a plan."

Col. Michael offered what comfort he could. "Mike, remember. There is an answer to every problem. Never give up hope."

CHAPTER THIRTY

On the Monday after the bonfire, everybody in school—except Darcy—waited for Mike to appear. She heard the buzz. Students and teachers alike wanted to congratulate him, to thank him for his hard work and leadership that led to the championship. When Mike didn't show up, they expressed understanding. Hey, the guy had played his heart out all season long. He hadn't missed a single game since Thanksgiving. He was always the first one at practice and the last one to leave. And he had accrued more playing time than anyone else on the team. All agreed Mike deserved a three-day weekend to recover.

By Thursday, people were expressing concern. Mike still hadn't returned to school, and no one had seen him anywhere around town.

Ms. Norman, Easton High's principal, called Darcy into her office. When Darcy entered, she was surprised to see Coach Hudson and Mr. Williams, the senior counselor, already there.

"Thank you for coming, Darcy," Ms. Norman said. "Please have a seat." She motioned toward a chair. "I'm sorry to take you out of class, but we thought perhaps you could give us some information concerning Mike."

Darcy sat down next to Coach Hudson, who sat slumped over, looking as though he'd lost the state championship instead of winning it. Deep lines creased his forehead, and there were puffy bags under his eyes. "Darcy, I've been trying for three days to reach Mike," he said. "Do you have any idea where he is?"

She shook her head.

Coach Hudson removed his ball cap and scratched his head. "I can understand if you're protecting him for some reason. But I've got college coaches and reporters calling me from all over the country. It would be to Mike's advantage to talk to them. Could be some big scholarship offers."

Darcy gripped the arms of her chair to steady herself. "The last time I saw or talked to Mike was Saturday night. I have no idea where he is."

Coach Hudson rested his elbows on his knees, his cap dangling from his hand. "I'm getting too old for this," he grumbled.

Ms. Norman turned to the counselor. "Sam, have you found anyone from Mike's past schools who might give us some information on his whereabouts?"

Mr. Williams' eye twitched behind his round, wire-rimmed glasses, and he stuttered as he talked. "Th-there seems t-to be a, uh, slight problem."

With her chin lowered, Ms. Norman peered over her half-lenses. "How slight?"

"W-well, it seems no one can, uh, locate his file. Wh-when we went to pull it...it was gone."

Now the principal leaned back in her leather chair and steepled her fingers in front of her chest. "What about our student data base? Any information there?"

The counselor crossed and uncrossed his legs and then studied his Hush Puppies. "Uh, th-there seems to be a problem there as well. S-some kind of glitch in the computer. All of Albright's information has been d-deleted."

"Well," Mrs. Norman said, "apparently Mike Albright has disappeared from the face of the earth." Her voice was low and controlled, but she was clearly agitated. She swiveled her chair around and stared out the window. "Thank you for all your *help*."

Along with the coach and counselor, Darcy scrambled from her office.

After a couple of days, Ms. Norman contacted the police, who interviewed teammates, teachers, coaches, friends—anyone who might have information concerning Mike's location. No one could shed light on his whereabouts. Without any evidence of criminal activity, the police couldn't request help from the FBI or other such agencies. They had to do what everyone else was doing—wait.

Darcy told the detectives the same thing she told Ms. Norman and Coach Hudson. She didn't know where Mike was. She kept from them what she did know: *Mike was alive, and they would never find him.*

CHAPTER THIRTY-ONE

Ever since their first meeting at MugShots, Darcy had lain awake nights trying to solve the puzzle of Mike's sketchy past. She hadn't asked many questions because she didn't want to appear nosy. But she'd listened. Words like *missions, service,* and *protection* came up in conversations. And she'd gathered clues. Mike's father left home often and for long periods of time, never disclosing his destinations. There was that mysterious meeting at Thanksgiving. Also, a guy as cute and athletic as Mike would make tons of friends anywhere he went. Yet he never spoke of former buddies or girlfriends. On Christmas Day, his lack of personal possessions had shocked Darcy. His room was empty of mementos from home or former schools. There were no pictures of family or any connections to his past life.

Adding to the mystery was the way Mike had vanished without a trace. The morning after their breakup, Darcy had driven out to the farmhouse to talk with Aunt Rosie. She got out of her car and shuddered at the eerie atmosphere. The few animals Aunt Rosie had kept were gone, even the big black dog which always lounged on the front steps. The window boxes, which had held spring flowers only days before, were full of dried weeds. Darcy peeked through a dusty window into the living room and gave a cry of alarm. There was not a stick of furniture to be seen. It was as though the place had been abandoned for years.

For a moment Darcy thought she had taken a wrong turn, come to the wrong house. Then she backed away from the window and saw it. The Flexible Flyer was propped in the corner of the porch. A note was attached: Return to Darcy Dunn.

She finally fit all the puzzle pieces together. Mike's dad was involved in a highly specialized branch of the government or military and participated in top-secret operations. Mike had been sent to Easton for protection while his dad carried out a dangerous assignment. But when Darcy broke up with him, Mike requested a transfer. He severed all ties with Easton and with her, and officials erased any evidence of his life there. With the government hiding him, Mike would never be found.

Knowing this eased Darcy's concern for Mike' safety, but nothing could ease her torment over losing him. Day in and day out, she performed her minimal duties like a robot. She went to class, played tennis, did homework, went to bed. Megan was the only friend she talked to—and seldom to her. Each morning Darcy threw on a pair of jeans and a sweatshirt, not bothering with her make-up or hair. What did it matter? There was no one to look good for. Incomplete college applications stacked up on her desk. Darcy couldn't care less *where* she went to college or even *if* she went.

Her parents tried every tactic in the psychology books to help her "snap out" of her depression. At first they were sympathetic and supportive. They told Darcy they knew how she felt...that everyone experiences heartbreak at some point in life but it seldom proves fatal. When passing weeks brought no change, they tried "tough love." They told her she was "ruining her life over a silly teenage crush" and it was "time to move on." When this approach proved no more effective than their initial one, they temporarily backed off. They let her live her life, just going through the motions. But Darcy knew her parents. They would never totally give up. If a few more weeks brought no improvement in her emotional state, they would seek professional help.

One night after an especially dismal dinner, Darcy lay on her bed and stared at the ceiling. Rufus was curled up beside her. These days she was sure he was the only one who understood how deeply she was hurting.

Her mother's words followed a light rap on the door. "Darcy... honey, we need to talk."

Oh, no. *Another* talk. Well, she might as well get it over with. The only way she would keep her mother from barging in would be to padlock the door. "Come in, Mom," she grumbled.

Her mother entered and sat on the edge of the bed. In silence she surveyed the chaos in the room. The look on her face wasn't necessarily one of disapproval, but Darcy knew what was going through her mind.

Darcy liked to display lots of reminders and souvenirs of the good times in her life. Pictures of her friends and posters of celebrities and professional tennis players covered her walls. Medals and award certificates hung there as well. Her bookcase was crammed with books and tennis trophies. Never immaculate, the room normally reflected what she called "orderly clutter." But tonight it looked like the aftermath of a fraternity party. Clothes and underwear were piled on every flat surface, including the floor. Her bed, which hadn't been made in weeks, was a tangle of rumpled blankets and sheets. On her desk were piles of paper and stacks of dirty dishes. A layer of dust covered everything.

She figured she'd save her mother the trouble. "I know," she said. "My room's a pigsty."

"Yes, it is. But that's not what I was thinking."

Okay, she'd take the bait. "Then what *were* you thinking?" she asked dismally.

"I was looking at all the evidence of your life to this point. Everywhere in here, I see reminders of how much you have going for you. You have family and so many friends who care about you. You have beauty and brains and incredible athletic ability." Her mother smoothed the wrinkles from the bedcovers next to her. "Darcy, your dad and I are at a loss as to what to do. You've had setbacks in your life before, but we've never seen you as devastated as you are by this one."

Darcy stared wide-eyed at her mother. "Mom, is that what you think I'm going through? A *setback*? Why is it so hard for people to understand what I'm feeling?" She choked back sobs. "Would you call a death in the family a setback? Is that what a divorce would be? Just because I'm young, why do you and my friends think this is not tearing me apart?"

Her mother placed her hands in her lap and studied them for a long while. Then she spoke softly. "I'm sorry, Darcy. I admit that up to this moment I've underestimated your loss. I guess I thought because you're young, you couldn't feel love or heartache so strongly. I was wrong." She placed her hand on her daughter's shoulder. "I truly believe time will heal your pain. But you've made me realize only you can determine how much time that will be. I haven't been fair in deciding that for you." She gave Darcy's shoulder a gentle squeeze and stood to leave. "Take all the time you need."

"Mom, wait." Darcy turned her face to the wall, unable to look at her mother. Tears trickled off her nose and onto the pillow. "I know my misery is dragging down everyone. And I hate that. But what you have to understand is this zombie-like existence is my only defense. If I don't have to think...about school or tennis or college...or anything... I don't have to *feel*. And if I don't have to feel, maybe" —her voice caught in her throat—"maybe I'll survive."

CHAPTER THIRTY-TWO

At school, Darcy noticed most of the Sevens had given up on trying to lift her spirits. At first, they continued to ask her to go out with them even though she always refused. The one time she did go to lunch with them, she was so dejected they all ended up eating in silence. Finally, like her mother, they backed off and gave her space.

But one person refused to let Darcy wallow in her self-pity. At school, Megan chatted non-stop, most of the time carrying on a one-sided conversation. Darcy would try to hide, but like a relentless bloodhound Megan tracked her down. She called Darcy faithfully every night, sometimes two or three times. Darcy rarely took her calls, but Megan didn't give up.

At the end of every school day, Megan showed up at Darcy's locker, trying to draw her back into the land of the living. One Thursday afternoon, as Megan rambled on about the most mundane events, Darcy pleaded with her. "Please, leave me alone. Can't you see? I don't care. I don't care who's dating Eric Miller, I don't care what new store opened at the mall, I don't care about cheerleader tryouts. Don't you get it, Megan?"

Darcy spoke slowly, distinctly pronouncing each syllable. "I. Don't. Care." She didn't want to hurt Megan, but she had to put an end to this constant badgering.

Megan ignored Darcy's tirade. "Do you care about the prom?"

Darcy rolled her eyes. Prom was the least of her concerns. How could she drill this concept into Megan's head? She assumed a bored expression and spoke in monotone. "What prom?"

"C'mon, Darcy, you know very well what prom. The same prom

every senior girl has been talking about since January. The one that's coming up in a week. The same prom you've been dreaming about since you were a freshman." Megan pounded her fist against the locker door. "Dang it, Darcy," she shouted. "It's the only senior prom you'll ever have in your entire life!"

Darcy watched Megan stomp away. *Good. She finally got it.*

Minutes later, Darcy stood outside Coach Davis's office and knocked timidly on the door.

"Come in," Coach Davis called out.

Darcy bit her lip and entered his office. Her coach wasn't going to like what she was about to tell him, but she had put it off as long as possible. "Coach," she mumbled, avoiding his eyes, "I'm quitting the team."

Coach Davis stopped his paper shuffling and looked up. "Excuse me?"

"I...I'm sorry," she continued. "But I wanted to tell you before practice today, so you could rearrange the line-up for tomorrow's tournament."

The coach scowled. "Let's talk about this." He nodded toward a chair.

Darcy didn't take his offer to sit. She hoped she wouldn't be in the office long. "There's not much to say. I know you've noticed my playing has dropped off the last few weeks. I don't want to play anymore, and I feel my attitude is hurting the whole team."

Coach Davis leaned back in his chair. "Darcy, I know Mike's disappearance has been hard on you, and I can understand why. I'm not so old that I don't remember the pain of breaking up." He rested his hands on his stomach. "You're a talented athlete and an excellent tennis player. But of all the qualities I've admired about you, your dedication to your teammates always impressed me most. Many people think of tennis as an individual sport, but you've always understood the concept of doing what's best for the team."

Darcy kept her head lowered. She didn't want to hear this lecture, but she guessed she had no choice.

"I don't need to explain to you what your quitting will do." The coach talked in a calm manner, but his disappointment in her was apparent. "You're our number one player. If you leave, I have to move each girl up to a harder position—one she's not prepared to play." He tapped a pencil on his desk as he thought. "I also don't have to explain to you how hard your teammates have worked. You of all people know the misery of playing through the summers in searing heat or in freezing temperatures in the winter. You know about playing through the pain of bleeding blisters or strained muscles. What makes it all worthwhile is the thrill of doing well at state. If I have to re-arrange the whole lineup, the other girls who've worked so hard don't stand a chance."

Darcy sniffed and wiped her eyes. If the coach wanted to make her feel guilty, he was doing a good job. But right now it took every ounce of her energy and determination to drag through the school day. She couldn't concentrate on her playing, and the thought of traveling to tournaments in a van full of cheerful, chatty girls repulsed her.

"Let's do this," Coach Davis said. "The van leaves for the tournament at six tomorrow morning. Skip practice today and think about what you really want to do. If I don't see you in the morning, I'll have your answer."

Darcy didn't go directly home. She drove to the tennis courts and parked where she wouldn't be noticed. Sitting in her car, she watched her teammates run drills, practice serves, and play out points. At the end of practice, their faces were flushed and their clothes were soaked with sweat. But they were smiling and joking and bumping fists.

The next morning at 5:50, Darcy loaded her tennis gear onto the school van and settled in for the two-hour drive to the tournament.

CHAPTER THIRTY-THREE

On Saturday, the Dunn's' doorbell rang at 9:00 AM. From her bed, Darcy heard her mother open the door. "Come in, Megan." Darcy groaned and pulled the covers over her head.

Five seconds later, Megan stormed into Darcy's bedroom. "We're going shopping. Prom is next week, and you don't have a dress. You can get up and get ready, or I can drag you to the mall in your pajamas. Makes no difference to me."

The set of Megan's jaw told Darcy she wasn't kidding. Slowly, she rolled out of bed and tugged on some jeans and a tee shirt she picked up off the floor. She brushed her teeth, splashed some water on her face, and pulled a ball cap over her scraggly hair. She gave Megan the same bored look she had used in their argument at her locker. "Okay, let's go."

On the way to the mall, Megan rattled on and on about the kind of dress Darcy should buy, the shoes she should get, the way she should wear her hair. Finally, Darcy managed to get in a word. "Megan, you're overlooking one minor detail here. I don't have a date to the prom." With a trembling voice, she added, "And I can't imagine going out with another guy even if he asked me."

"I know that. I've already thought about it. You're going with Chad and me." Darcy opened her mouth to argue, but Megan cut her off. "I'm not taking *no* for an answer. I've already talked this over with Chad, and he's all for it. You know he loves you as much as I do." Megan grinned. "Anyway, we've been together so long we're like an old married couple. Having someone else around will give us something new to talk about."

At the mall, Darcy flipped through racks of formals, not giving

149

them much more than a glance. With prom only a week away, the dresses were picked over, but she didn't care. This prom "date" was more for Megan than for her.

They found nothing at the large department stores, so Darcy and Megan checked the mall directory. A new dress shop had opened in a remote corner of the complex.

Darcy didn't expect to find anything but was surprised to find the perfect dress, a strapless gown of royal blue. Frothy layers of ankle-length tulle flowed from a dropped-waist, form-fitting bodice of shimmering satin. She stepped from the dressing room and modeled the dress for Megan.

"That's the one," Megan said without a moment's hesitation. "That style makes you look like a super-model. And the color makes your eyes pop." She grinned and nodded encouragement. "So are you saying "yes" to the dress?"

Darcy returned the nod and paid for the gown. Then she and Megan searched other stores for accessories. They left the mall and walked toward Megan's car loaded down with packages. Darcy realized it had been over an hour since she'd thought about Mike.

"A bunch of us are going to Chad's tonight for pizza and a movie," Megan said on the drive home. "Want to come?"

Darcy thought for a moment. "You know, as much as I hate to admit it, this has been a good day for me. In fact, the best one I've had since Mike left," she added quietly. "But I'm not up for a party yet."

"That's okay. I didn't expect you to come, but thought I'd ask anyway." Megan kept her attention focused on the road and nodded her approval. "You did good today. I'm proud of you."

Darcy took a long look at her friend. Sitting on a pillow, she craned her neck to see over the steering wheel of her subcompact and drove ten miles over the speed limit. The corners of Darcy's mouth twitched and then broke into a smile. She thought back to when she and Megan had first met.

The day of the bus incident, Darcy had rushed home and gone straight to her room. She almost wished the bus had hit her. If she complained to her parents, they would contact the school, and that might keep Tiffin off her case for a while. But it wouldn't get Darcy what she wanted most—a friend. Someone her age to talk with, to laugh with, to commiserate with. Someone to assure her she wasn't the loser Tiffin insisted she was. With one person like that, she could survive middle school. Darcy didn't know what else to do, so she prayed. She prayed for a friend.

The next week, her math teacher assigned partners for a project. She paired Megan and Darcy together, and they bonded immediately. Megan introduced Darcy to some of her friends, and the Sevens were formed. Megan gave Darcy the acceptance she so desperately wanted at this new school.

At the first of this year, Darcy had doubted a guardian angel would save her. Now she realized she hadn't needed one. In middle school and again today, her best friend had rescued her from a sadness that threatened to destroy her.

Despite her heart sickness, Darcy hadn't missed a day of school since the night Mike disappeared. But in homeroom on Monday, it was as if she'd been absent for weeks. Changes occurred she hadn't noticed before: The desks were re-arranged, the chubby girl at the back of the room had lost weight, the boy with the shoulder-length hair now sported a buzz. But the biggest change was in Tiffin.

This morning, as Tiffin and Reese walked in late together—some things never changed—Tiffin said nothing. Downcast eyes and a drooping mouth replaced her usual ear-to-ear smile.

And Tiffin's style had changed. In past springs, Tiffin wasted no time in breaking out her summer wardrobe whenever the temperature soared to over sixty degrees. She'd sit in class and shiver in her short shorts and low cut tank tops. But today she wore cropped pants with a tee shirt and jean jacket. A scarf was knotted around her neck.

"Is this a new look for Tiffin?" Darcy whispered to Megan.

"She's been dressing like this for a couple of weeks." She raised her eyebrows and shrugged.

Tiffin's make-up was different, too. She was now wearing it heavier as impossible as that seemed.

This morning Reese walked Tiffin to her desk with his hand clamped around the back of her neck. She didn't speak to any of her friends. She averted her eyes when she passed Darcy.

But Darcy looked at Tiffin. And what she saw was sadness and defeat. For a moment, Darcy felt sorry for her. Then she remembered the night of the bonfire.

CHAPTER THIRTY-FOUR

Darcy caught herself humming as she soaked in the tub. The steamy, scented bubble bath helped calm the misgivings she'd had about tonight. She lingered until the water turned tepid, then she climbed out and slathered on citrus-scented body lotion. It had been weeks since she cared about her appearance. But this afternoon, as she got ready for the prom, she was enjoying the little rituals she used to perform.

Darcy gave herself a pedicure and manicure and spent thirty minutes doing her make-up. She brushed smoky grey shadow over her eyelids, smudged charcoal liner on the rims, and stroked on two layers lash-extending mascara. Then she blended a creamy blush onto her cheekbones and tinted her lips with a pale rose color. A touch of gloss in the center made her lips shimmery but not greasy. For the finishing touch, she lightly bronzed her forehead, her chin, and the tip of her nose.

Darcy inspected her make-up, her face two inches from the mirror. She backed away and scrutinized the overall effect. Satisfied with the results, she moved on to her hair.

To compliment the simple cut of her gown, Darcy decided to wear her hair up, but not in those fussy, stiff curls that looked like lacquered sausages. Instead, she knotted it up in back and secured it with a rhinestone clip. In the front she parted it on the side and formed a soft bang. Loose tendrils fell around her face.

She checked the mirror again. The look was coming together.

Her mother knocked on the door, then stepped into the room. "Lookin' good," she said. "I love your hair.. Is there anything I can do?"

"In a minute. I'll need some help with my dress."

Darcy put on her jewelry—rhinestone earrings that hung almost to her shoulders and a two-strand rhinestone bracelet. The bracelet brought a sharp stab of memory—the memory of another bracelet, lost to her forever. She quickly pushed the image of the star bracelet from her mind, refusing to undo the emotional progress she had made over the past week.

She slipped her polished toes into silver and rhinestone sandals with three-inch spiked heels. By the time she left the prom, her feet would be killing her, but these shoes were worth the pain.

Her mother helped her step into the gown and smoothed the folds of the skirt. When she zipped it , the dress fit as if it had been custom made.

"You're breathtaking," Mom said. She arranged a stray wisp of Darcy's hair. "I'm so proud of you."

Darcy turned in front of her full-length mirror, pleased with what she saw. It dawned on her she hadn't felt this good in a long time. Then another wave of sadness washed over her. She remembered the way Mike had looked at her the night of the Harvest Moon Dance. It would have been wonderful to look this way for him tonight.

Darcy carefully arranged the skirt of her gown into her car and drove herself to the country club, where the prom was being held. Megan had argued that she and Chad would come by and get her, but Darcy flatly refused. She didn't want to tag along with them all night like somebody's wallflower cousin. Besides, she'd have Bee there to make a quick getaway if she wanted to leave early.

Darcy fought back doubts as she drove. This was all wrong. In all her adolescent fantasies about this night, she had never envisioned driving herself. Alone.

She indulged in one last regret about Mike then ordered herself to let it go. This night was for Megan, her friends, and her parents. She'd once heard that you can think yourself into a way of acting, and you can act yourself into a way of thinking. Tonight she would test that theory by acting as if she was having fun.

Cars packed the lot at the country club, so Darcy had to park near the back. Even in this remote spot, she could hear the music. The band had its amps in overdrive. The noise inside could probably shatter eardrums, but hearing the thumping, bone-jarring bass put Darcy in a dancing mood. Maybe tonight wouldn't be so bad after all.

She didn't want to keep up with a purse all night, but before she locked it away, she tried calling Megan. She needed to find out where to meet up with her. All she got was Megan's voicemail.

"Great," Darcy grumbled. Picking out Megan among the glittering mob would be like finding a diamond in a tub of crushed ice. She put her phone into her purse and tossed them both into Bee's trunk.

Walking toward the club, Darcy heard other noises, but they weren't sounds of celebration. Curses, followed by slaps and cries of pain, came from somewhere in the parking lot.

She looked around but didn't see anyone. Her pulse throbbed in her throat as she walked. The sounds were growing louder and more violent. She stepped to the front of a black pickup and stopped. Her hand flew to her mouth, and her eyes grew wide at the scene before her.

On the pavement, Tiffin clambered to her hands and knees. Make-up streaked her face, and blood trickled from a cut at the corner of her mouth. A strand of hair fell over a swollen, purplish eye. She struggled to crawl away from Reese who was staggering toward her, but her legs and feet were entangled in her ripped, sequined gown.

Tiffin's pleas of "Don't" and "Leave me alone" gripped Darcy's heart. Reese's nasty, degrading insults knotted her stomach.

When he reached Tiffin, Reese kicked her from behind. The impact sent her sprawling face-first onto the concrete. Blood oozed from a scrape on her chin. She lay there sobbing, too hurt and frightened to move. He drew back his foot to deliver another blow.

"Reese! Stop!" Darcy yelled.

Reese turned toward Darcy. He wobbled from side to side and blinked his bloodshot eyes as he tried to focus. "Get out of here, Darcy," he slurred when he finally recognized her. "Mind your own business. This is between me and Tiffin."

Drops of sweat broke out on Darcy's face as chill bumps formed on the rest of her body. She choked back the bitter, acrid bile rising in her throat. Her eyes went everywhere in a frantic search for help, but no one was in sight. It was useless to shout. No one in the noisy ballroom would hear her. *Why hadn't she brought her phone?*

Reese caught Tiffin by the arm and dragged her across the concrete. Like a wounded animal caught in a trap, she kicked and writhed to free herself. But despite his drunken condition, Reese was too strong for her to break his grip.

Darcy stood by helplessly, paralyzed by horror and disgust. From out of nowhere, the question came to her: "If I don't help her, who will?" With a jolt, she understood what Mike had meant when he spoke those words.

Hatred for Reese and compassion for Tiffin gave Darcy courage. No matter what Tiffin had done in the past, she didn't deserve this. *No girl* deserved this.

Darcy searched for a weapon. Anything...something sharp...something pointed—her shoe!

Darcy kicked off both shoes and grabbed one of them. She charged at Reese and pounded his head and face with the spiked heel. Reese, drunk and confused, held up his arms to protect himself. Then he swayed and fell backward.

Seizing the opportunity, Darcy sprinted toward Tiffin and grabbed her around the chest. "Get up, Tiffin. Get up!"

Tiffin rose shakily to her feet. Darcy looped Tiffin's arm over her shoulder and put her own arm around Tiffin's waist. "Run!" she screamed, and they scrambled to Darcy's car.

With Tiffin in the passenger seat, Darcy tore out of the parking lot, making a turn on two wheels. In her rearview mirror, she saw Reese stumbling toward his truck. Above the band's ruckus and the hum of her motor, she heard him hurling obscenities and threats of getting even.

Darcy was torn between relief and panic. She and Tiffin had escaped, but she was sure Reese was chasing them at this very moment. She sped toward home. Her parents would know what to do.

The two girls rode in silence until they reached the vacated stretch of road near Darcy's house. Darcy heard Tiffin's moans. "Hang on, Tiffin," she said. "We'll get you help at my house."

Tiffin leaned forward and clutched her stomach. Then she placed her hands over her face and sobbed. The sobs gave way to wails.

Darcy recognized the sounds. They were the same ones that had come from her at this very place not so long ago. She recalled the crushing pain, the complete sense of hopelessness that accompanied them.

All of Darcy's hatred toward Tiffin melted. How had she missed the signs? They had certainly been there. But Darcy had been so caught up in her own fears of being bullied, she hadn't recognized Tiffin was running from a bully herself. Mike's disappearance had left Darcy with a broken heart, but it had left Tiffin with no hope of escape from an abusive, controlling monster.

"Tiffin, I'm so sorry. I had no idea..." Darcy glanced over at Tiffin and put her hand on the girl's shoulder. Then she looked back at the road just in time to see the deer.

Darcy gripped the steering wheel with both hands and slammed on the brakes. Tires squealed, the car swerved to the right, and the front wheel dropped off the pavement onto the shoulder. Darcy tried to correct the problem, but she lost control. The little yellow car rolled three times before coming to a stop. Upside down.

* * * *

"Is something wrong, sir?" Mike asked.

"You need to return to Easton immediately."

In all but the most trying circumstances, Col. Michael maintained his level-headed, assuring composure. Tonight his urgency alarmed Mike. "I can't give you all the details right now. There isn't time." In brusque military style, the colonel continued his orders. "All the arrangements for your departure have been made."

"Yes, sir. I'll leave right away." Mike was aching to ask if he'd found a solution to his problem. But he knew it was useless to ask any more questions.

As Mike departed, the colonel addressed him once more. This time he spoke as a loving father to a son. "Mike, I once told you we can't always control our circumstances or feelings. But we can choose our reactions to them. You'll have the answer to your question in Easton."

CHAPTER THIRTY-FIVE

Hidden from view, Mike listened in the emergency room as two policemen tried to give Darcy's parents an explanation. The officers said something about an accident, an overturned car, and two teenage girls. Carol's and Chet's stunned expressions indicated none of this made sense to them.

Later, two doctors—a neurologist and an internist—visited with the Dunns. They explained Darcy had sustained extensive hemorrhaging in both her body cavity and in her skull. A CAT scan revealed a ruptured spleen which required immediate surgery to remove. The extent of her head injuries couldn't be determined until the bleeding stopped and the swelling subsided. Within twenty-four hours, the doctors would know more, and they could tell the Dunns something more definite.

Chet drew his wife to him. "Darcy will be fine," he tried to assure her. "Try to think—"

"I can't!" Carol shouted. "I can't think." Then she covered her eyes with her hand and spoke in a whisper. "Darcy once tried to explain this to me. If you don't have to think, you don't have to feel. I didn't understand at the time, but now I do."

Carol rested her head on Chet's shoulder. "So I'm not going to think. I won't think about the day Darcy was born and how happy I was to find out I had a baby girl. I won't think about all the *firsts:* the first step, the first day of school, the first tennis lesson, the first date. I won't think about shopping with Darcy, arguing over hemlines and exchanging fashion tips. I won't think about the two of us riding in the car, singing off-key to a tune on the radio and laughing. I won't think about the all the ways Darcy has blessed my life. And I won't think about how empty my life will be without her."

All of Carol's fear and anxiety escaped in sobs. Chet held her close and offered what comfort he could, but his voice was tight and strained.

After a while, she drew a jagged breath and spoke again. "The doctors said we would know something in twenty-four hours. In twenty-four hours, I'll know if I'm to spend the rest of my life happy and whole or with a part of me missing. So for the next twenty-four hours, I'm not going to think."

Mike continued to watch the Dunns as they agonized through the hours of surgery. He watched them as they followed Darcy's gurney from the operating room to the intensive care unit. When Darcy was settled in a room, Chet tried to persuade Carol to leave. "There's nothing you can do for the next few hours. Why don't you go home, get some rest, eat something? I'll be here if anything changes."

Carol refused, so Chet made plans to go himself. First, he would go to the hospital lobby and report Darcy's condition to the crowd of friends and students gathered there. Word of the accident had spread quickly, and many came as soon as they heard to offer support, prayers, and blood if it was needed. After that, Chet would go home to feed Rufus, clean up, and eat. He would bring Carol a change of clothes and some food when he returned.

Now, Mike watched Carol as she sat by Darcy's bedside in the cold, sterile room of the ICU. She sat in a chair positioned at the head of a bed with her back erect and her shoulders rigid. Her hands lay stiffly in her lap, and she stared without blinking at the mangled body before her. Her only action was the slight movement of her lips as she prayed. Then just before daybreak, she left the room.

A labyrinth of tubes and wires originated from machines with assorted dials and knobs and ended somewhere under the sheets or beneath Darcy's bandages. The only sounds in the room were Darcy's labored breathing and the bleeps and ticking from the impersonal, uncaring machines.

Mike recalled Col. Michael's words: "You'll have your answer in Easton."

At last, Mike knew.

CHAPTER THIRTY-SIX

"Darcy. Darcy..."

Darcy flailed her arms in slow motion, suspended in a gelatinous sea. Above the surface of the water, a man silhouetted against a brilliant light called to her.

"I'm coming...I'm coming," Darcy moaned. "I'm almost—"

Darcy opened her eyes. She blinked to erase the disturbing images that occupied the foggy region between sleep and consciousness. Images of her car rolling over...a scream...the sound of sirens...Tiffin.

As the fog lifted, Darcy determined she was in a hospital room. On the other side of a glass, a nurse at a hallway desk read a computer screen and made notations on a chart.

Darcy couldn't move any of her limbs, but she could turn her head slightly. She surveyed the room, taking in the strange and frightening surroundings. When her survey reached the foot of her bed, she gasped. She closed her eyes to shield them from the figure that stood there. A figure made of light and fire.

"Don't be afraid," the luminary said.

Darcy recognized the voice and opened her eyes. A mixture of elation and tranquility replaced her fear. Everything would be okay. *Mike had returned.*

Mike walked to the head of the bed. His body took on its familiar appearance, and he gently laid his hand on Darcy's shoulder. "How are you feeling?"

To an observer, this question would sound absurd. From all indications, Darcy should have been in enormous pain, but she wasn't. "Fine," she said. "A little confused."

"Well, maybe I can clear up some of that confusion." Mike drew the chair close to the bed and sat down. He leaned forward and rested his elbows on his knees. "Do you remember Valentine's night when I told you someday I'd answer all your questions? I'm here to do that now, but you have to listen with an open mind. You have to believe this first thing I tell you, or nothing else I say will make sense."

"I'm listening."

"Darcy, my real name is Michelangelo. I'm an angel."

Darcy's heart raced, but the beeps on the heart monitor remained constant. The nurse at the desk continued her duties, giving no indication anything was wrong.

She took her time processing this information. At first she thought Mike was joking, but his serious tone and the absence of a smile told her otherwise. Then she thought Mike had lost his mind. Or maybe she'd lost hers. But she lay there recalling the events and experiences of the past few months. As crazy as it sounded, his claim seemed credible.

The same facts which led her to believe his dad worked for the government fit this explanation even better. And other things made sense as well: his superhuman abilities on the basketball court, those haloes that appeared out of nowhere, his innocence when it came to so many "earthly" matters.

Right now she should be in incredible pain, but wasn't. If this absence of pain was due to drugs, her thoughts would be muddled, not clear and lucid. And she should have been frightened instead of experiencing this strange sense of peace.

What overshadowed all these "facts," though—what was most convincing of all—was Mike's extraordinary goodness. Darcy had always thought Mike was too good to be human.

Darcy weighed the evidence and came to the only logical conclusion. "I believe you," she said.

Mike released a huge sigh. "Good. With that out of the way, I can tell you more." He talked in the matter-of-fact way an engineer or an accountant might explain his duties. "Just as people have different jobs to do, so do angels. Some angels worship God, some protect people. That's what I do, Darcy. I protect people. I'm a guardian angel."

Darcy noted the machines to which she was tethered, the tangle of tubes and wires, the bandages. "Don't be offended, Mike, but I think you need some more training."

He smiled. "Yes, I can see why you'd think that. But I wasn't *your* guardian angel. I was *Tiffin's*."

Another wave of shock surged through Darcy. She lay still, not moving a muscle. Then a horrible thought occurred to her. "There was an accident. Tiffin was there. You were—"

"Tiffin is fine." Mike smoothed the panic from Darcy's face. "Thanks to you, she's fine. She's already been checked out and released from the hospital. She suffered a few minor injuries, but most of those came from Reese. You saved her life. In more ways than one."

In bits and pieces, events from the previous evening came back to Darcy as she replayed the horrible scene between Tiffin and Reese in her mind. She regretted her suspicion and jealousy over Mike's concern for Tiffin. All that time he'd only been doing his job.

Mike reached for Darcy's hand and enclosed it in both of his. "The night of the bonfire I couldn't bear to see how much I'd hurt you. I ran after you. I wanted to explain...but you disappeared into the crowd. And I had to leave. My orders were to report back to headquarters that night."

"You left." Darcy's tone was one of disbelief rather than accusation. "Without a word, with no explanation."

"I had no choice. In my work, I can't question orders. I don't always see the reasoning behind them, but failing to follow orders can have disastrous results." Mike paused and drew a deep breath. "When I was first told to return home, I asked for an extension. I didn't feel my mission was completed. You'd think by this time I would learn not to doubt, but sometimes it's hard to obey when you can't see the entire picture.

"The whole time I was in Easton, I thought Tiffin was my assignment and mine alone. I thought I had to protect her until she learned to take care of herself. I kept looking for a change in her—some maturity, wisdom—something to indicate she could make it on her own."

Mike stared across the room at a blank wall, his mouth pressed into a thin line of self-reproach. Then he shook his head and released a humorless laugh. "I couldn't have been more wrong. My assignment was to take care of Tiffin only until God sent someone to take my place." He shifted his eyes to meet Darcy's. "That someone was you."

"Me? You must be joking. God used me to—" She stopped when

she realized that was exactly what happened. Months ago, when she had vowed to *take care* of Tiffin, this is not what she'd had in mind. Darcy saw a knowing smile spread across Mike's face.

"You see," he said, "angels can't be two places at once. But when angels aren't there, God uses humans...brave ones, caring ones... like you."

"Angels can't be everywhere? I thought angels worked miracles."

"A lot of people think that. But God works the miracles, and they are mostly miracles of the human heart. He knew your heart would change. He foresaw your ability to forgive, to see Tiffin for what she was —a frightened girl searching for someone to help her."

These words swirled in Darcy's head. This was too much for her to sort out right now, and she had a bigger concern. One she was almost too frightened to mention.

"Mike—" her mouth went dry with fear— "does this 'picture' you talk about include a future for you and me?"

CHAPTER THIRTY-SEVEN

To Darcy, it seemed an eternity passed before Mike spoke.

"It does. But not in the way you might expect." He sat back and ran his hand through his hair. "You see, angels and humans are not of the same species. Angels are spiritual beings. We experience many of the same emotions as humans, but we don't have physical bodies unless we need them for an assignment on Earth."

He pinched the bridge of his nose. "Maybe I can explain it this way. Do you remember Christmas Day at Aunt Rosie's?"

"The day you gave me the bracelet." Darcy smiled dreamily. "There were so many people...every age, size, shape, race..."

"You remarked that surely all those people couldn't be from the same family."

Darcy remembered how strange it had all seemed. "So what you're saying is all those people were members of an...'angel family'... wearing the 'bodies' they needed to do their earthly jobs."

"That's right."

"And Aunt Rosie. An angel, too?"

"An angel, too. Aunt Rosie—Rosangela—came to help me after I found out how much trouble Reese was going to cause.

"She was also the guardian angel who rescued you from the bus collision. The form of an old lady allowed her to perform her duty without calling attention to herself. My duty was to protect a teenage girl. Like Rosangela, I was given the form which seemed best suited for the job. So while you think you love an eighteen-year-old guy, you have no idea who—or what—I am."

"I have a confession," Darcy said. "Maybe if you hadn't been so gorgeous, this whole predicament would have been avoided. I'm as superficial as the next girl. Your 'form' was what first attracted me to you in the first place. It didn't take long, though, for me to recognize how amazing you are. I'd never known anyone like you. You were so genuine, so good. And you were always kind to everyone."

She managed a chuckle. "I'd love you now if you looked like a villain in a Batman movie. You have a beautiful spirit, and it's your spirit I love."

Mike lowered his head. "I have a confession, too. In our conversations, I've often talked of a dad or father, but those are terms I use only on Earth. Col. Michael is the closest thing I have to a father. The affection between us is much like that between an earthly father and son, but he's actually my commanding officer. When he ordered me back to headquarters, I begged for more time in Easton. Told him I wanted to finish the basketball season with the team." Mike raised his eyes to meet Darcy's. "That was the truth, but there was more. I didn't want to leave Easton because of you. When I did report back, I told Col. Michael how much I loved you. I thought perhaps…somehow…he could work out something for us."

"Did he?" Darcy forced the words from her tightened throat.

"Yes. But I didn't know it until tonight."

Mike rose and walked across the room. He stood with his back to Darcy, his head bowed, his shoulders slumped.

"I came tonight fully expecting to take you home with me," he said. "I didn't know how, but I was convinced there was a way."

He straightened his body but continued to face away from her. "Before I made myself visible, I wandered through the lobby. Your friends from school and church and work had gathered there. I heard them say how much they loved you and what you meant to them. I've never seen Megan so sad." He chuckled. "For the first time in her life, she was at a loss for words." His voice grew grave again. "Then I saw the torture your parents were going through. How could I take you away from so many people who loved you? Angels are supposed to encourage, comfort, and protect people. How could I be the cause of so much pain?"

"But what about me?" Darcy asked. "What about my pain?"

He turned to her. "You said you know my spirit. Well, I know yours, too. You would never intentionally hurt anyone. You stayed on the tennis team because you didn't want to let your friends down. You went to the prom to make Megan and your parents happy. And you risked your life to rescue Tiffin. Earth needs people like you. I would be selfish beyond belief to take you with me."

Darcy felt herself freefalling into the same darkness that had engulfed her after Mike's disappearance. She had climbed once from that desolate abyss. Not sure she could do it again, she grasped at a lifeline. "Mike, I love my parents and my friends. But I love you, too. I shouldn't have to choose. There must be a way for us to be together. Can't you stay here? On Earth?"

Mike returned to the chair and sat on its edge. His eyes shone and his voice shook as he spoke. "You remember I said angels are spiritual beings?"

Darcy nodded.

"And you are human. God has created each of us with our own special features and abilities. He has placed us where can best serve Him. For me, it's the spirit realm. For you, it's Earth." He paused and swallowed hard. "Darcy, I can't stay here. And I can't take you with me."

Darcy couldn't breathe. Anger pounded her chest, and pain coiled around her heart, threatening to crush it. This was all so unfair. She had put others' feelings before her own. She had risked her life to save Tiffin. Now it was as if she was being punished for doing what was right.

"Mike, I love you," she said. "When you left, my heart—my whole world—collapsed. I didn't think I would ever be happy or feel complete again. If there was no way we could be together, why were you sent back? Just when I was starting to recover, why torture me again? Why remind me of what I lost?"

After a long silence, Mike said, "I think it's because...He wanted you to be sure."

"He? Sure of what?"

"I told you I'm a guardian angel. But the word *angel* means messenger. And I have a very important message for you. Do you remember the question I always asked you?"

Darcy remembered. Mike had asked it a thousand times. Until the night of the victory party—the night Mike disappeared—it had always taken her mind off her troubles. "Where would I go?" she whispered.

He nodded. "That first night we talked at MugShots, you told me you wanted to be somewhere—anywhere—other than Easton. You wanted to run away from your problems. So I made up the game. What was always your answer?"

"Beyond the farthest star."

"Why such a vague response? Why couldn't you ever decide on a specific destination?"

"Because..." Darcy probed her mind for the answer. "Because I didn't truly know where I wanted to be."

"That's right," Mike said. "You didn't know because you weren't searching for a place. You were searching for Darcy—for who and what you are. And that's the message I have for you."

Mike's words grew intense. "Who you are, Darcy, is a caring and brave and selfless person. But more importantly, you are a child of God."

He drew his face close to hers and Darcy felt his warm breath on her cheek. "Your recovery will be slow and sometimes difficult. God wants you to know He loves you and will see you through it. But here is the exciting part. You *will* recover. And when you do, God has a plan for your life—a wonderful plan to give you a future full of hope. That future includes helping thousands of people in ways you can't imagine right now. That is going to happen right here on Earth...in Easton...where you are desperately needed."

Darcy blinked back her tears. "Mike, whatever is good or brave about me is because of you. I'll always love you. I can never forget you."

"Trust me, Darcy. You won't always love me. With time, people heal, move on. But you're right about the other. You won't forget me. Not completely."

Mike smiled sadly and caressed Darcy's cheek with the back of his hand. He choked back a sob as he spoke. "In the not- too-distant future, I will be no more than an airy notion in some obscure corner of your mind. A misty memory that rises and then vanishes as quickly as it came." He rose slowly and stood by the bed. "But what you will remember every day of your life with absolute certainty is God loves you. You will have a constant reminder of that."

Darcy turned her head away from Mike. She believed him. Her heart would heal. Someday. But for now, she feared if she looked at him for one moment longer, it would shatter into a million pieces.

"Goodbye, Darcy," she heard him say, and a touch as light as a feather swept across her wrist. Then Mike's words became a fading echo.

"Always remember who you are and Whose you are. God will take care of you. And I'll be watching you forever. From beyond the farthest star."

A radiant light filled the room, and Mike was gone.

* * * *

Darcy viewed the hospital room between the narrow slits of her eyelids. A throbbing in her head prevented her from thinking about how she got there.

"Welcome back, sweetheart," someone said, and a soft hand soothed her brow.

Her mother stood beside the bed. Her face was tired, but she smiled through her tears.

"Mom," Darcy murmured. "What happened? Why am I here?"

Her mother explained what she knew of the previous night's events. There were gaps in the story, but Darcy was too weak to ask questions.

Darcy had a sense of Mike having been in this very room, and she recalled the words of comfort and encouragement he'd spoken. For a fleeting moment, a blanket of peace enveloped her. Then reality set in, and she dismissed the experience as effects of the drugs she'd been given. The medicine could bring relief from physical pain, but she resigned herself to living forever with a dull hurt in her heart.

Mom stood beside the bed softly stroking Darcy's arm. She suddenly stopped, and a puzzled expression crossed her face. "I thought you lost this, Darcy."

Unable to lift her head, Darcy cast her eyes to where her arm lay limp beside her. On her wrist was a delicate silver bracelet. Its star charm glowed with a luster that seemed to come from within.

EPILOGUE

"Teen Crisis Center. May I help you?" The attractive, forty-ish director of the center answered the hotline and listened with concern. When the panicked caller finished, the director asked, "Do you have a way to get to the center?"

Hearing the answer she wanted, the director continued in a calm voice. "Listen carefully. Come to the center immediately. Do you know where we're located? Good. Don't take time to pack any clothes or toiletries. We have everything you'll need. And don't worry. You did the right thing to call. You'll be okay."

The director hung up and placed a call on another line. A teenage girl answered.   "Hello."

"Hi, hon. How was your day?"

"Fine, I guess. I left my math homework at home this morning, so I had to go in after school and re-do it. Then Mrs. Lusk assigned us a ton of reading in *Wuthering Heights*. I'm gonna download it and watch it on my phone, though."

"I don't think so. You need to *read* it. In fact, I'm going to ask you some questions about it tonight. Anything else going on?"

"Jess came home, and she's up in her room. She's trying to remove some nail polish she spilled, but I think she's mostly removing the color from the carpet."

"Wonderful. Go up and tell her to stop immediately before the whole floor disintegrates. I'll think of something when I get there. Is your dad home yet?"

"Not yet. And, Mom, I have a drama club meeting tonight. We're re-writing a scene from *A Midsummer Night's Dream*. We're going to do it as aliens from a neighboring galaxy."

"Should be interesting. Listen, I might be a little late. I've got a new client coming in. Go ahead and start dinner without me. I should be home before you leave for your meeting, so I'll see you then."

"Okay."

"Jordyn?"

"Yeah, Mom?"

"I love you."

"Me too, Mom. Bye."

"Good-bye."

The director leaned back in her chair and smiled. All day long she heard from teens with huge problems—problems even adults shouldn't have to face. She knew how alone and hopeless these young people felt, and she did all she could to help them. But for Tiffin Spencer, it was comforting to know that sometimes, somewhere in this universe, there were crazy teenagers doing mindless teenage stuff.

About The Author

Dee Dee Chumley

Dee Dee Chumley taught high school English for over twenty years, coaching girls' tennis eleven of those. Currently, she spends her "retirement" pursuing her passion for creative writing, reading, traveling, and enjoying an occasional game of tennis. She lives in Edmond, Oklahoma, with her husband Bill and rescue dog Jack.